Healing the Souls of Black Men

Dr. Wayne C. Cooper

ISBN: 979-8-89122-408-7

Dedication

To the Black men of the past, present, and future,

This book is dedicated to you—to the kings who carried the world's weight on their shoulders and yet still stood tall, to the sons who seek their place in a society that often misjudges their worth, to the fathers who have fought to provide, protect, and nurture in the face of relentless storms, and to the brothers who have lifted each other up when the world sought to tear them down.

You are more than the labels imposed upon you. You are strength, resilience, wisdom, and love. You are the heartbeat of a community, the legacy of a people, and the vision for a brighter future.

This book is a tribute to your pain, perseverance, and potential. It is a call to healing, to reclaiming the wholeness that has been denied for far too long. May these words serve as a balm to your soul, a beacon of hope, and a testament to the undeniable truth that you are seen, valued, and deeply loved.

This is for the Black men who dare to heal and for the generations who will rise because of it.

Secondly, I thank my beloved father, Mr. Leon E. Cooper, Sr., whose love and nurturing presence in my formative years became the foundation upon which I built my life. Your wisdom, strength, and unwavering belief in me have left an indelible mark on my soul. Though you are no longer with us, your legacy lives on in every step I take.

And to my late father-in-law, Pastor Lee R. Baker, a warm, loving, and kind human being who exemplified what it means to be a true Christian leader. Your guidance, encouragement, and gentle spirit embraced me when I was still finding my way as a young man. Your faith in me gave me the confidence to become who I am today. Thank you for taking me under your wings and showing me what leading with love and compassion truly means.

Preface

The soul of a man is a sacred space - a reservoir of experiences, emotions, and dreams. When I set out to write *Healing the Souls of Black Men*, I was driven by a singular, unyielding conviction: the struggles and triumphs of Black men in our society must be recognized, understood, and, most importantly, addressed with the urgency and empathy they deserve. This book is not merely a reflection on the pain that has been endured but also a blueprint for recovery, a testament to resilience, and a call to action for all those who seek to heal and be healed.

The experiences of Black men are unique, shaped by a history of systemic racism, social and economic disenfranchisement, and cultural marginalization. Yet, within these struggles lies a strength passed down through generations. The soul of a Black man is forged in fire-tempered by adversity, yet enriched by an unbeatable spirit, vibrant culture, and a legacy of resistance and perseverance.

As a Black man, I have seen firsthand the struggles that come with navigating a world that often misunderstands and misrepresents us. The burdens of systemic racism, economic disparity, and societal expectations weigh heavily on the shoulders of Black men, often leaving scars that are difficult to heal. Yet, amid these challenges, there is resilience, a strength forged in the crucible of adversity, a determination to survive, and an unwavering desire to thrive.

Healing the Souls of Black Men is not merely a recounting of pain but a celebration of healing. It is a guide for Black men and those who love them to navigate the complex landscape of mental health, emotional wellness, and spiritual growth. It recognizes the intersectionality of race, gender, and identity, offering insights and strategies for healing that are rooted in cultural understanding and compassion. Healing, as I present it here, is not a one-size-fits-all solution. It is a deeply personal journey - one that calls us to confront our past, embrace our present, and envision a future where we are whole and fulfilled.

As you read through these pages, I invite you to reflect on the stories and strategies shared and consider how they resonate with your own experiences or those of the Black men in your life. Whether you are a Black man seeking to understand and heal your own soul, a family member, or an ally wanting to support the Black men around you, this book is a guide - a beacon of hope that healing is possible and begins with understanding, compassion, and the courage to confront even the most painful truths.

Let this book be a step toward healing, of individual souls and of the collective spirit. Together, we can break the cycles of trauma, nurture our communities, and create a world where Black men are not only surviving but thriving.

Table of Contents

About the Author

Dr. Wayne C. Cooper proudly hails from Tampa Bay, Florida, specifically the charming city of Tarpon Springs. As the fourth of six children, he embodies the values of family and resilience. With eleven years of dedicated service in the U.S. Army, Dr. Cooper was honorably discharged in 1989, a testament to his commitment and discipline. His journey took a transformative turn as he embraced his calling to Christian ministry, leading him to seek higher education at several esteemed institutions. In May 2024, he earned a Doctor of Ministry degree in Spiritual Formation and Soul Care from Talbot School of Theology at Biola University in La Mirada, California. For three decades, Dr. Cooper and his family have thrived in Southern California, enriching their community. His extensive travels across Europe, Asia, the Caribbean, and North America have broadened his perspective and deepened his understanding, enhancing his ability to inspire and lead.

Page Left Blank Intentionally

Chapter One

Historical Trauma and Resilience

In the depths of history, the souls of Black men have endured a profound and complex journey. From the horrors of slavery to the relentless fight for civil rights, the narrative of Black men in America has been one of both resilience and struggle. Nevertheless, amidst the external battles waged against them, there lies a profound internal struggle - a battle for healing and wholeness that has too often been overlooked. Within this context, *Healing the Souls of Black Men* takes root, a profound exploration into the unique challenges and transformative potential inherent in the Black male experience.

This book is an unapologetic invitation to delve into the depths of Black masculinity, where vulnerability meets strength, wounds are acknowledged and transformed, and the possibility of healing lies. With a compassionate lens, we embark on a transformative journey into the inner lives of Black men, exploring their struggles, fears, hopes, and aspirations. In doing so, we shed light on the intricacies and complexities of their existence, exposing the profound impact of systemic oppression, societal expectations, and personal traumas.

Healing the Souls of Black Men seeks to dismantle the stereotypes and misconceptions that have long perpetuated the marginalization and oppression of Black men. It creates a space for healing, growth, and empowerment by honoring the richness of their stories and recognizing the multiplicity of their experiences. Within these pages, we encounter the narratives of Black men from various walks of life, sharing their truths, triumphs, and journeys toward self-discovery.

Drawing on the wisdom of psychologists, sociologists, and scholars, this book offers a comprehensive exploration of the factors that shape the lives of Black men. It delves into the intersectionality of race, gender, and identity, examining how these dimensions intertwine to shape their experiences. Additionally, it challenges the notion of a monolithic Black male experience, recognizing the vast diversity within this community and the importance of honoring individual narratives.

Healing the Souls of Black Men also extends an urgent call to address the mental health crisis disproportionately affecting Black men. It exposes the detrimental effects of toxic masculinity, the burden of unresolved trauma, and the barriers to seeking help, which are deeply rooted in historical and cultural contexts. By illuminating these issues, this book seeks to foster empathy, understanding, and a collective commitment to breaking down the walls that hinder healing and growth.

Ultimately, this book stands as a testament to the steadfast spirit and resilience of Black men. It celebrates their strengths, contributions, and capacity for love, growth, and transformation. It serves as a rallying cry for communities, policymakers, and individuals alike to come together, dismantling the oppressive structures that hinder Black men from realizing their full potential. Through these pages, we aim to create a space where healing can flourish, where Black men can find solace, support, and the empowerment needed to reclaim their souls and rewrite their narratives.

As we embark on this journey together, we must listen, learn, and unlearn. We must challenge ourselves to see the world through new lenses, embrace the discomfort of growth, and uplift the voices that have long been silenced. Only then can we begin the sacred work of healing the souls of Black men and forging a future that honors their humanity, worth, and right to thrive.

This chapter of the study will examine the historical trauma experienced by the African American population, with a specific focus on Black men. It will explore the historical experiences of Black men, including slavery, segregation, and systemic racism, and discuss how these events have contributed to collective trauma and resilience. The following section will present information on historical trauma and its impact on the life experiences of Black men.

Historical trauma is related to the generational impact that slavery had and lingers in the lives of Black men. Historical trauma is often referred to as posttraumatic slave syndrome (PTSS) (Burrowes, 2019; Halloran, 2018). PTSS is described as "a condition that exists when a population has experienced multigenerational trauma resulting from centuries of slavery and continues to experience oppression and institutionalized racism today." (Burrowes, 2019, p. 2). While slavery itself was not the direct experience of today's Black men, the reality is that the negative impacts of slavery have a transgenerational effect on Black men in the United States (Pough, 2019). Black men of today have heard their great-grandparents share the experience of slavery, and these stories have been passed down through generations of Black families for several centuries, which has left an impact on the minds, emotions, and conceptualizations of the world around them. The trauma of slavery hangs like a dark cloud over Black men, affecting their personal and collective conceptualization of themselves and the world around them, often making them feel lesser than their White counterparts - a feeling further exacerbated by systemic discrimination.

Humans are fundamentally shaped by the environment in which they grow and live, and families, churches, schools, and society shape the individual (Pough, 2019). Being forced into slavery alone is enough to impact generations of families emotionally and mentally, creating problems that Black men continue to cope with in today's world. However, the experience of being forcefully sold into slavery and transported to a foreign land profoundly and negatively affected the psychological mindsets, social standing, and perceived limitations among Black men. Although slavery and segregation in schools no longer exist, the psychological effects continue among Black males in the United States, influencing their perception of who they are and what they are capable of achieving (Pough, 2019). The psychological state, mentalities, and lifestyles of the Black slave ancestors having been passed down through generations of Black families, continue to harm Black men today. Black men in America understand that they are the descendants of slaves, which often leads to feelings of shame and embarrassment, emotions they carry with them throughout their daily lives (Pough, 2019).

Moreover, research studies on this problem "have been shrouded in secrecy and stigma, with any associated emotion being pushed away" (Pough, 2019, p. 4). Therefore, not only are Black men carrying that burden but it has also not been well-acknowledged in research, creating a tenuous situation for the individuals and their experiences. Instead, this problem and experience for Black men after the days of slavery morphed into structural racism that is deeply ingrained in society (Scott-Jones & Kamara, 2020).

For example, research indicates that the Black-White color line in cities has continued (Logan, 2013). This Black-White color line is also evident in rural areas in states such as Alabama, where the Black population lives in specific areas separate from the White population. Generally, these areas are plagued by environmental problems. For example, in the state of Alabama, a small town, once home to slave labor in the cotton fields, has become the site of a toxic waste disposal facility. Hazardous material has been dumped there, which has been the case in many places throughout the southern United States where a prejudicial pattern has been noted (Wilson, 2023). Specifically, "communities where hazardous waste disposal facilities are located also share similar demographics, such as social class and racial/ethnic composition," and it has been noted in various studies that a significant relationship exists between the proportion of racial minorities in communities where toxic waste sites are located (Wilson, 2023, p. 2). Another example of toxic waste that has disproportionately affected Black communities is along the Tennessee River in Lawrence County, Alabama, where large industrial sites have dumped waste into the river near the Black neighborhoods.

Although segregation may seem like a thing of the past, systemic racism continues to confine much of the

Black population to areas that are unhealthy, contributing to increased health problems and mortality rates. Furthermore, structural racism was clearly evident in the days of slavery, and it is still deeply ingrained into the very fabric of the lives of Black men (Scott-Jones & Kamara, 2020). For example, Black men face ongoing economic disadvantages and health disparities, and the persistent trauma they experience affects how they view themselves and their life situations. The experience of racism, which has been defined as the attitudes, actions, beliefs, and institutional arrangements that work in denigrating groups or individuals, has been a constant experience for Black men since approximately the 17th century. The problem began when millions of Africans were forcibly shipped to the Americas and sold into a life of slavery, referred to as the African Diaspora. Those individuals experienced family separation, loss of identity and names, experienced rape, beatings, and torture. African Americans were marginalized within the institutions and systems of the United States. That marginalization continues today in the form of structural racism, wherein there is a "normalization and legitimization of an array of dynamics that stem from historical, cultural, institutional, and interpersonal aspects that routinely advantage Caucasians while producing cumulative and chronic adverse outcomes for people of color" (Scott-Jones & Kamara, 2020, p. 2).

Historically, there has been significant prejudice among mental health providers toward Black Americans, and they are over-diagnosed with mental health problems, such as schizophrenia, and given antipsychotic medications, which can have long-term adverse effects. Moreover, African Americans experience depression at the highest rates but are treated at the lowest rates (Scott-Jones & Kamara, 2020). Research indicates that Black men have what is termed 'vacant esteem' or the lack of development of the individual's primary esteem, resulting in feelings of depression and hopelessness because they do not feel their inherent value. For Black men, Vacant esteem can manifest in harmful ways, including a belief that they do not deserve healthy monogamous relationships. To compensate for these feelings, many may seek to bolster their self-esteem through behaviors that align with stereotypical notions of masculinity in terms of how many women they sleep with rather than focusing on achieving socioeconomic goals, particularly in situations of economic strain (Scott-Jones & Kamara, 2020).

The perceptions Black men hold of themselves are highly influenced by what the world around them says about them, driving the toxic masculinity that this book discusses or the idea of what it means to be a man. Black men often perceive societal expectations as diverging from the principles of what they believe God has called men to be in their lives and communities. It has been noted that Black men are under pressure to project dominance, aggression, and strength (Teti et al., 2012).

Additionally, Black men often perceive the world around them with suspicion, feeling that others are negatively motivated. This perception can result in violence directed toward others, themselves, property, or even their own family rather than acknowledging the systemic barriers stemming from oppression and systematic racism, and they may blame African American women (Scott-Jones & Kamara, 2020). Socialized in an environment marked by racism, Black men may develop behavioral problems, such as a distorted self-concept, learned helplessness, and extreme aversion or antipathy toward their own ethnic or cultural group and its traditions. In turn, this may result in idealizing white values and norms. However, structural racism is certainly problematic for African Americans in today's world, and it impacts Black men and their conceptualization of the world and their place in it (Scott-Jones & Kamara, 2020).

However, there is a better way forward, and this book intends to guide Black men toward realizing their potential through self-determination rooted in Jesus Christ and a better understanding of their true identity. This book intends to lead Black men toward the ultimate freedom that comes from Christ, breaking the invisible chains that still bind many and providing the strength and purpose needed to navigate the real, systemic barriers of structural racism. By doing so, Black men can become strong and empowered men in their personal lives, family, community, and the wider society. This book intends to support Black men in embracing their unique abilities and strengths to make a difference in their lives and the world around them.

It is not possible to examine historical trauma without understanding the collective victimhood experienced by the Black population and the resilience it has built among Black men. According to Selvanathan et al. (2021), "collective victimhood and collective resilience are two sides of the same coin" (p. 136). A prominent example of resilience among the Black population, widely known, is the Underground Railroad, which emerged in the 1800s during the slavery era. The Underground Railroad was characterized by a network of places, such as barns, homes, and churches, designed to assist in freeing thousands of enslaved people from the Southern United States. The Underground Railroad is one example of how hardship and victimhood gave rise to resilience among African Americans. As the Black population was subject to collective victimization, the experience made the population more aware of their victimization and how they interpreted the harm that arose from that experience. As the Black population became more aware of their collective trauma, it gave rise to psychological resistance, as social support networks formed within the African American groups during slavery. The historical narratives of slavery are integral to African Americans' collective memory, and the way they remember their past has a significant effect on the identity of the group and its sense of who they are in the world. Resilience arises as the group makes sense of its social environment and creates a shared social reality. The result is that,

"Social representations of history are, therefore, intertwined with the broader political and social system within which an individual lives... they may specifically draw on their history of collective resilience to provide a sense of collective continuity in the context of responding to ongoing experiences of oppression" (Selvanathan et al., 2021, p. 140).

Research shows that the collective memory held by African Americans of overcoming slavery makes provision for a primary lens through which the Black population understands their collective identity (Selvanathan et al. 2021). The fight against oppression within the Black population has been a long one, shaping values and actions of collective in-group resilience. This resilience acts as a buffer against the adverse outcomes of collective victimhood. However, the ending of slavery and the supposed ending of segregation did not end the discrimination that Black men and the entire population of African Americans have suffered.

For example, during the Civil Rights Movement, the assassination of Martin Luther King, Jr. created a hallmark moment in the lives and minds of African Americans. The same is true for the 1955 incident when Emmett Till was brutally killed for supposedly making sexual remarks toward a White woman. Emmett Till was just 14 years old and was visiting family in the South, unaware of the extent of racism that still existed. White men kidnapped the young Emmett, and while they were arrested and charged, they were found not guilty of the murder. These events have become deeply ingrained in the minds of Black men, and despite the horrors suffered and the ingrained racism and systematic exclusion, Black men and the entire population of African Americans in the United States have developed remarkable resilience. In the study of Selvanathan et al. (2021), 81.25% of Black participants attributed resilience to the struggles arising from racism and adversity, emphasizing the development of collective strength and empowerment.

From Rosa Parks's stance during the Civil Rights Era to the promotion of self-determination by the Black Panther Party, the experiences of Black men have formed a profound and significant resilience to the experiences that have been suffered and are ongoing for Black men.

National reports in the United States have highlighted that Black men are endangered, disadvantaged, invisible, left behind, or in crisis (Teti et al., 2012). Black men are more likely to drop out of school, experience poverty, or face incarceration. Additionally, they have the highest mortality rate of any ethnic, gender, or racial group in the United States. A study was conducted to examine the experiences of Black men in the United States, and it involved interviewing 30 participants between the ages of 18 and 44, revealing that most participants had low incomes and 50% were unemployed. Interviewees described their lives as tough and challenging. One participant revealed his experience as a Black man and stated his life was "a constant struggle... always a constant oppressor." (Teti et al., p. 527). Another participant revealed that "every day feels like a different struggle." (Teti et al., p. 527).

The participants revealed the difficulties associated with four interrelated socio-structural challenges that compounded their difficulties, including incarceration, racial micro aggressions, unemployment, struggling to support their families, and coping with the stress of the streets. Racial micro-aggressions were described as daily encounters with demeaning messages, indignities, insults, and the perception of feeling worthless. One participant shared how "it was hard for him and other Black men to be taken seriously because people expected him to do nothin' with my life... Go to jail like everybody else...want nothing for my future... Be a lowlife." (Teti et al., 2012, p. 527). However, another participant revealed how those microaggressions and societal expectations felt like "a noose around [his] neck." (Teti et al., 2012, p. 528). Despite these overwhelming challenges, the participants in the study emphasized their resilience because they talked about how they kept on going by persevering in the face of those challenges. One participant revealed the following:

"[There are] two strikes against me: I'm Black, and I'm [an] ex-felon. So you settle like, Okay, you can't make it further than what we [society] allow you to. And like me myself, I can't get stuck in that. You know, I can't get stuck in that, 'cause there is so much out here for me as a Black man, so much... Basically, if I apply for [a] job, an' they shut the door, I just go apply for another one better than that one. For instance, I went on three interviews in one day… Keep goin,' keep goin,' I keep goin'." (Teti et al., 2012, p. 528).

Despite the struggles faced by Black men in the study, their unwavering focus on resilience and the understanding that they must 'keep goin' is remarkable. This determination highlights the deep and abiding resilience among Black men as they struggle in an environment that continues to be characterized by systemic racism. This integral resilience has been ingrained into the Black population during their previous struggles with slavery, struggles that have been woven into the collective trauma and resilience of the population. Teti's (2012) study also emphasizes the awareness among Black men of the transformative power of education as a means to overcome their struggles and break free from the chains of poverty and ignorance. Rising above the challenges and systemic racism is characterized well throughout the United States as Black men have risen to achieve great things despite the struggles that exist for them in the world around them.

One compelling example of resilience is the story of Ben Carson. Carson's mother married at 13 and dropped out of school, and by the time he was eight years old, his parents divorced (Achievement.org, 2024). His mother was forced to leave her two sons to work two and often three jobs to make ends meet. By the time he was in fifth grade, Ben Carson had fallen far behind in school and was at the bottom of his class. His classmates called him names such as 'dummy,' and he struggled with an uncontrollable temper. However, his mother was determined to address the issue. She implemented strict rules at home, limiting television time, prioritizing homework, and requiring him to read two library books weekly.

This turning point came when Ben Carson read a book on rock samples and shocked his class by identifying the rock samples the teacher had presented in class. He suddenly realized he was not stupid. With newfound confidence, Carson worked hard to improve academically, rose to the top of his class and decided to become a physician.

Having gained control over his temper and excelled in school, Carson attended Yale University, earning a psychology degree. He then went to the University of Michigan Medical School. He became a neurosurgeon at Johns Hopkins in Baltimore, Maryland. He made history in 1987 when he conducted an operation and successfully separated a pair of (Siamese) twins. Ben received the Presidential Medal of Freedom in 2008, awarded to him by then-President George W. Bush. The life of Ben Carson is an example of how resilience, despite the struggles against systemic racism, poverty, and family issues, promotes Black men to overcome challenges and succeed. In his book *Gifted Hands*, Ben Carson noted that the creator has endowed everyone with unique abilities and how it is crucial that every individual get in touch with that aspect of themselves or their intellect, develop it and move into careers that allow them to use their intellectual talents and abilities. Carson stated, "There is no such thing as an average human being. If you have a normal brain, you are superior" (Achievement. Org, 2024, para. 1).

Ben Carson is just one example of a Black man who came from poverty, a broken family, and low beginnings ascended to remarkable success by nurturing his intellectual potential through education. Carson had a strong Black woman as his mother, who drove him to achieve educationally, and he rose above his situation and the systemic racism that exists in today's society

(Achievement.org, 2024). However, there was a moment in his life when he realized he was not stupid and could achieve, and unfortunately, many Black men have never had the opportunity to experience these types of moments (Achievement.org, 2024). This chapter sets the stage for the book by revealing the historical trauma and resilience of Black men, illustrating the deep-seated struggles and triumphs that have shaped their collective experiences. The following chapter will examine the identity and self-perception of Black men. It will explore how Black men perceive themselves within the context of societal expectations and stereotypes, information that is briefly touched upon in this chapter but examined in depth in Chapter Two.

Chapter Two

Identity and Self-Perception

This chapter will explore how Black men perceive themselves within the context of societal expectations and stereotypes and how cultural pride and heritage shape identity. The following section will examine how Black men perceive themselves within the context of societal expectations and stereotypes.

Black Men's Self-Perception and Societal Expectations and Stereotypes

In the field of psychology, according to Melson-Silimon et al. (2023), "stereotypes have generally been viewed as overgeneralized beliefs about social groups in society" (p. 1). Stereotypes cause very narrow and, at times, negative beliefs about the attitudes, behaviors, and characteristics of marginalized groups, that may lead to prejudice. For example, there is a stereotype that Black men generally cannot swim. However, historical examples of Black male swimming competitors show otherwise. This stereotype arose from the segregation of Black children from swimming pools during the Jim Crow Era, when swimming pools were privatized to keep Black children out, and the story is told that Black men cannot swim. Still, it fails to consider that they did not have the chance to swim for generations. The reality is that the slaves who were captured swam regularly before becoming slaves, and this story is a cover-up "for the longstanding systemic racism – racial oppression that is maintained through the policies and practices that make up an organization or society – that truly explains racial disparities in swimming and drowning rates" (p. 2). Therefore, the general orientation toward stereotypes fails to consider the impact of the social systems in which people live (Melson-Silimon et al., 2023).

Black men's perception of their identity has been influenced by the period of slavery, where Black people were sold and bought like livestock. Those supporting slavery justified it with the claim that Black people were not intellectually equipped to serve alternative roles within the larger society (Melson-Silimon et al., 2023).

Research seeking to back the stereotyping of Black people with evidence continued into the 20th century. Tools that had been developed, such as intelligence tests, were used to support the intellectual inferiority of the Black race. However, those same stereotypes persist in the present. For example, Black students feel anxiety about entering fields of study where they have been stereotyped as underperformers. Another stereotype that persists is the idea that Black individuals are mentally and physically strong, making them well-suited for hard labor. This stereotype carries on in today's society in various forms. However, the attempt to adhere to the stereotype of strength means that Black individuals believe they must suppress their emotions, which can result in anxiety and depression (Melson-Silimon et al., 2023).

Black males cope with multiple problems that affect their self-perception and social identity. Research shows that it is necessary to take an intersectional approach to understand identity (Buckley, 2018). The intersection between gender and race is shown to have an impact on adjustment among adolescents. In the United States, "being Black and male... may be particularly challenging in this regard. Black males are connected with a set of stereotypes and assumptions deeply rooted in the history of slavery, reinforced by media portrayals of Black male violence, criminality, and government policy – particularly around policing – that perpetuates these stereotypes" (Buckley, 2018, p. 2).

Gender Schema Theory combines cognitive theories associated with sex typing with cognitive and social learning theories to understand the person's readiness to use a gender lens as they view the world (Buckley, 2018). Central to this theory is the idea that people have varying feelings and thoughts about gender that affect how they perceive, regulate, and evaluate their behaviors and those of others. From a lens of gender, individuals tend to perceive themselves according to traditional stereotypes and what is deemed to be the appropriate attitudes and behavior. However, more theoretical research is needed on the gender roles of Black males, acknowledging how gender is constructed socially according to cultural and racial influences. Black Racial Identity Theory examines differences within racial beliefs, thoughts, and attitudes within groups, showing that these attributes among Black individuals are fluid and influenced by social context, geography, ego development, and age. The socially constructed identity based on those stated characteristics means that the Black male may experience positive or negative attitudes about racial identity (Buckley, 2018).

Social Identity theory, or the individual's self-perception, is partly derived from their feelings and experiences about belonging to a social group, which affects their self-concept (Buckley, 2018). For example, if the individual belongs to a social group at school or some other life domain and feels valued, their self-perception is more positive. However, within the context of school, social stereotypes have, far too often been driven by gender and race stereotypes, resulting in discipline for Black males that is harsh and supports the widespread idea that they perform poorly in academic achievement, which negatively affects their self-concept. Research supports the belief that Black males often "adopt a 'hyper-masculine' or 'cool pose' as a reactive strategy to offset the demands of a European American normative masculine ideal that may be too difficult to attain" (Buckley, 2018, p. 8).

Research also indicates that social imagery has shaped how people think about and perceive reality (Howard et al., 2012). Social imagery occurs through language, media, constructed knowledge, and experiences within a particular group. In the context of the United States, racial minority groups have had their experiences shaped via social imagery that has caused enormous hardships in the development of a healthy self-perception and self-actualization. Black males have been "one of the most primary victims of negative social imagery" (Howard et al., 2012, p. 86). The negative social imagery has severe adverse impacts on Black males. Research shows that Black males, throughout the range of K-12, do not meet grade-level proficiency in several subjects, and less than ten percent are at their grade level or exceed it. Black male students are more likely to be expelled or suspended from schools than any other racial group. They are more likely to be placed in special education classes or receive remedial services (Howard et al., 2012).

Racial stereotypes, social imagery, and beliefs about Black men are perpetuated early in the lives of Black males. These stereotypes affect Black men and how they perceive themselves in relation to the world around them. One example of how social imagery has impacted the self-perceptions of Black men is stated by Howard et al. (2012) as follows:

"Early 17th and 18th-century images typically cast Black men as physically strong, mentally inept, hyper-sexed brutes who were well suited for slavery and deemed to be subhuman. Over time, the image became more entrenched of Black men being lazy, docile, and inhumane savages. We have also witnessed the depiction of Black males as the Sambo or minstrel characters who only sought to entertain their superiors. Many of the twentieth-century depictions painted Black males as pimps, thugs, hustlers, and law-breaking slicksters who were not to be trusted, were not worthy of equal treatment, and needed to be marginalized because they were a 'menace to society,' prone to violence, and constantly involved in gangs and drugs. These characterizations have become entrenched in the public mind through pseudo-scientific research, literary sources of the day, cinematic outlets, and persistent caricatures. These caricatures contributed to the development of an image that perpetuates widespread disdain for Black men" (p. 89).

Intersectionality theory, according to Harris and Kruger (2022), "describes the ways interlocking systems of oppression shape one's experience," which may include gender, social class, and race, but rather than describing similar or different groups, encapsulates ongoing relations of material, political, historical, stigma and social inequality. Intersectionality theory also holds that systemic oppression based on social status, gender, and race is further exacerbated by the experience of the individual, emphasizing the different outcomes experienced by individuals depending on the identified factors. For Black males, gender does provide some advantages, although they exist in a state of continuous oppression due to racism (Harris & Kruger, 2022).

A study was conducted to examine how 12 Black males' perception of their gender identity was shaped and found that Black men had positive views of their gender identity, and even though they cope with historically based and present-day trauma, they can "thrive and maintain a strong sense of community" (Harris & Kruger, 2022, p. 557). However, the participants expressed how they perceived a negative view of themselves as Black men from other people and keenly felt discrimination. The responses were divided into high and low-prosocial groups. Among the low-prosocial groups, one participant stated: "Because you can see, in everything we do, we already got some hate thrown at us. Like most of the movies and shows on TV, it's White folks on there" (Harris & Kruger, 2022, p. 558). The participants revealed a belief that the view of the racially gendered identity was viewed by others positively only concerning specific Black men stereotypes: women and sports. One participant, identified as Ray and belonging to the low-prosocial group, stated the following:

"They pitch to us, like when we leave high school, sports gonna get us out. They don't pitch us as doctors or lawyers... they try to teach us to dumb us down, so that – because the Black man in power is – he's dangerous to everybody else" (Harris & Kruger, 2022, p. 558).

However, the men in the high prosocial group had a different view. For example, one participant in that group stated: "I see everybody the same. It's just that's what they see, what they perceive in the world as, and what you see may be different because so many people see their world in their own type of way" (Harris & Kruger, 2022, p. 559). Another participant in the high prosocial group stated, "Some people, and I'm not gonna label them as White people, they're cool people, I'm not gonna be like, 'Oh, that's a White person over there.' I'm trying to get past that" (Harris & Kruger, 2022). The participants in the study noted how their experiences of dehumanization and prosocial attitudes influenced their identity development. However, the participants stated that, due to their experience of oppression, they felt vulnerable and felt that, at times, they were unfairly tested to see if the stereotypes that society expresses are true (Harris & Kruger, 2022).

Du Bois (2023) wrote of the self-perception of Black men:

"But before that nameless prejudice that leaps beyond all this, he stands helpless, dismayed, and well-nigh speechless; before that personal disrespect and mockery, the ridicule and systematic humiliation, the distortion of fact and wanton license of fancy, the cynical ignoring of the better and the boisterous welcoming of the worse... but the facing of so vast a prejudice could not but bring the inevitable self-questioning, self-disparagement, and lowering of ideals which always accompany repression and breed in an atmosphere of contempt and hate" (p. 6).

Many Black men inevitably carry a negative self-perception based on the social imagery, stereotypes, and systemic racism that is deeply ingrained in the world around them. Research has shown that, even when Black men excel, they may experience something referred to as 'imposter syndrome' or a feeling they do not belong and only gain their position or achievements by luck. It is necessary, however, to consider imposter syndrome from the perspective of clinical psychology (Cokley et al., 2024).

Imposter syndrome involves embedded distorted cognitions and has been linked to heightened levels of depression and anxiety, as well as low self-esteem, indicating that imposter syndrome reflects a pattern of thinking that is distressed (Cokley et al., 2024). Imposter syndrome is particularly evident among Black men who excel in college. For example, one study examined the experience of imposter syndrome among Black male doctoral students and defined imposter syndrome as "a psychological condition with a pattern of beliefs held typically by accomplished people who secretly feel like frauds" (Chakraverty, 2020, p. 434). The study found that imposter syndrome causes Black individuals to feel a lack of a sense of belonging, exacerbates complications associated with intersecting identities, and amplifies the experience of stereotyping (Chakraverty, 2020). Black men are shown in the research to experience 'racial anxiety,' characterized by a feeling of "discomfort about the potential consequences of interracial interactions. Black men and boys often experience the anxiety that they will be the subject of discrimination or hostile or distant treatment" (Perception.org, N. D., p. 12). Stereotyping has been shown to cause physiological changes in the brain and body, particularly placing Black men at a heightened risk for cardiovascular problems associated with suppressing the feeling of self-doubt (Perception.org, N. D.). The self-perception of Black men is significantly influenced by stereotypes affecting their educational achievement and life trajectory (Perception.org, N. D.).

In summary, Black men experience discrimination based on their race and gender that infiltrates society and the world they live in through educational institutions and is perpetuated by Hollywood films and other media. Various theories have been espoused to explain how race and gender intersect among Black men, along with socioeconomic factors. It is difficult for Black men to escape those stereotypes, and, even when they successfully do so, they may experience imposter syndrome, feeling as though they do not belong in the role or position they have achieved. Black men face so much in their daily lives related to racism and stigma that, understandably, their self-perspective is negatively affected. When Black men are from lower socioeconomic classes, their self-perception is further harmed. In a society that views Black men negatively, perpetuated by faulty stereotypes, it is not surprising that Black men often feel defeated at early ages, even before they have truly begun to develop as students and members of society. The following section will examine the role that cultural pride and heritage play in shaping the identity of Black men.

The Role of Cultural Pride and Heritage in Shaping the Identity of Black Men

In the United States, the African American culture, or Black culture, is referred to as:

"the cultural contributions of African Americans to the culture of the United States, either as part of or distinct from American culture. The distinct identity of African American culture is rooted in the historical experience of the African American people, including the Middle Passage. The culture is both distinct and enormously influential to American culture as a whole" (Brown, 2013, p. 57).

The culture and heritage of African Americans are deeply rooted in Africa, which blends the Sahelean and sub-Saharan cultures, and although slavery interfered with those cultural practices, across time, the values, beliefs, and practices have survived in some form and have blended with other cultures, such as those of White people and Native Americans (Brown, 2013). The African culture entailed elaborate ceremonies and rituals based on spirituality and the belief that death was not the end of existence. Black people of today have all but lost their connections to traditional African culture, but during the era of slavery, they developed their own unique African American culture. When slavery began early in the 17th century, societal marginalization and physical isolation caused some of the significant characteristics of traditional culture to be lost. However, African Americans did retain some significant elements of their traditional culture. The cultures of Africa, slavery, rebellion among slaves, and the civil rights movement have all served to shape the familial, religious, economic, and political behaviors of African Americans (Brown, 2013).

The African American culture is deeply embedded in religious worship because preachers tend to do more than only speak; emotion is integrated into the way and cadence of how they speak (Brown, 2013). The African American heritage and culture are also embedded in the oral traditions passed down because of the limitations that slaveholders put on African Americans receiving education, fearing that it would lead to an uprising against slavery. The oral traditions served to preserve the culture, history, and practices of the African American population, ensuring the stories were passed through the generations. Through the lens of slavery, African Americans developed their unique cultural traditions, much of which had to do with suffering and hardship while overcoming the challenges they faced in their lives. Spirituality and worship helped the slaves escape from their downtrodden existence as they worshipped God, who promised them freedom from the bondage of sin (Brown, 2013).

The African American culture follows the beliefs, practices, and customs of the traditional African culture based on the belief that the individual can only survive if the group survives, a feature of communalism that involves an interconnectedness between the individual, others, and nature, including spirituality (Johnson & Carter, 2020). Research has shown that there are theoretical differences in the theories on Black racial identity; however, their membership in the racial group affects their behavior, thinking, and affectivity. Using the Multidimensional Inventory of Black Identity (MIBI) and the Black Racial Identity Attitudes Scale (BRIAS), research has shown that African Americans have positive thoughts about belonging to the Black race and see it as crucial to their identity. Racial socialization is revealed to involve how direct and indirect messages surrounding race among African Americans have raised an awareness about oppression and supported the development of cultural pride that is shared within the African American community by parents, family, and members of the community. Those racial socialization messages are interconnected “with racial identity status attitudes, presenting a cyclical pattern between the two. Studies show that racial socialization occurs more frequently when the receiver has high internalization attitudes and racial pride” (Johnson & Carter, 2020, p. 60).

Positive Black cultural values emerged despite the contact that African Americans had with White individuals because the Black population developed methods to deal with the oppression (Johnson & Carter, 2020). The Black population sought social support in group-centered activities. Cultural pride reinforcement involves pointing the children of Black families toward acknowledging their cultural strengths. The specific themes emphasized to African American children include how their culture and heritage help promote survival in American society, the crucial aspect of education to advance in society, and preparing for the blatant and subtle experiences of racism they will face (Bannon et al., 2009). The role that racial socialization plays has been examined by developmental theorists to understand how it affects the outcomes of minority children (Bannon et al., 2009). When parents reinforce cultural pride messages, it has been shown to positively impact youth outcomes, including self-esteem and anger control (Bannon et al., 2009).

A study examining how Black males in the college setting described the development of their Black identity involved interviews with participants who had graduated from HBCUs between 1989 and 2010 and had attended graduate school (Rogers & Mitchell, 2022). Eight participants were in the study, and six revealed having a Black male role model during their life outside of the immediate family. One of the participants described that being a Black male meant they had a connection to their ancestors, strength, and spirituality and stated:

"Being a Black male just means, number one, I'm a man of strength. I think based on heritage and things we've gone through over a number of years; I've just noticed the strength of Black men overall is particularly strong. I see a lot of Black men in terms of how they try to overcome a lot of resistance and are resilient, and basically just try to make a strong mark in today's society" (Rogers & Mitchell, 2022, p. 2257).

Another participant described his identity as a Black male and revealed that he knew at an early age that he had to strive harder than others and stated:

"I grew up in the South, so I would say at least kindergarten. You knew that in kindergarten or preschool, you knew you were different... I mean, we were always different. You understood, and you wanted to be better. So, I guess it's something that at an early age has always been there" (Rogers & Mitchell, 2022, p. 2258).

Another participant revealed this about the development of cultural pride as follows:

"I've always been a Black male, but I think really getting into what it means to be a Black man, I would say high school, tenth-grade year. My ninth-grade year, I went to a Catholic private high school, which was a mixed population but majority white. I went there, and I went to some public school. So the public school, I'm not sure how the public school got teachings from the Afro-centric perspective... I think from there, I really developed a sense of pride, a sense of history, and a knowledge about myself, and my community. That's really where I fully got tuned into being a Black man" (Rogers & Mitchell, 2022, p. 2258).

As the participants in the study developed their identities as Black males at very young ages, a sense of pride developed about their cultural heritage. The participants noted that attending an HBCU was integral to developing their cultural identity and pride (Rogers & Mitchell, 2022). One participant noted that:

"Your network is your net worth, and if you're proud and you are being the man you're supposed to be, your network should be vast. And so, I think for a Black male, you need to be a good father. You need to be a good worker and contributor. And the type of person that people seek out for assistance. And they're comfortable with seeking out your assistance. And you take pride in assisting others. And a father to all, not just, 'Oh, this is my child.' Any room I walk into and there's kids in there, I feel like a father, and I accept the responsibility to be that. And I think a proud Black man accepts the responsibility of everybody" (Rogers & Mitchell, 2022, p. 2260).

The participants stressed that Black males must know who they are and who they represent because they represent more than just themselves in the world around them (Rogers & Mitchell, 2022). The participants noted that they had strong role models in their lives in the form of other Black men, whether it was their father, a coach, or a professor in college, which helped them recognize the importance of becoming role models for the younger generation. One participant stated as follows:

"The knowledge and acknowledgment of my history and of our history... So it's a matter of teaching the next generation, 'This is what happened, this is what can happen,' and get them to understand it, teach them to learn from our mistakes, and that there are certain things you just don't want to find out for yourself" (Rogers & Mitchell, 2022, p. 2269).

The participants revealed that they felt responsible for guiding the next generation to ensure their ancestors' legacy is continued. Specifically, "We have a responsibility first to guide them to our ancestors... We're not here because of what, anything we've done. It's all because of those who came before us, and we have to carry on that legacy" (Rogers & Mitchell, 2022, p. 2270).

For Black men, embracing cultural pride and their heritage builds strength, enabling them to draw upon their ancestors' experiences and the teachings of their culture to strive to be better than the stereotypes perpetuated in society. However, there is a need for strong Black male role models in the lives of young Black men to point them in the right direction and to guide them in becoming all they can be as individuals, as family men, and as members of society, which points toward the communality in the Black culture and heritage that provides direction and strength to Black men.

Chapter Three

Breaking Stereotypes

As already revealed in previous chapters, Black men cope with stereotypes, which negatively impact their self-esteem and social interactions. Far too often, Black men embrace those stereotypes, which perpetuates them in society and causes Black men to fall far short of what they can achieve and be in the world. However, overcoming those stereotypes and displaying different qualities to the world around them can assist Black men in creating a new narrative about who they are. This chapter will examine the strategies for challenging and redefining those stereotypes.

One example of a widely accepted stereotype in the United States is the idea that Black males are innately athletic and possess physical ability and strength (Melson-Silimon et al., 2023). The problem arises when Black males in sports are presented as being intellectually inferior despite their physical gifts and are dehumanized, affecting Black males because, often, as boys, they internalize those stereotypes and see that sports might be their only way to achieve economic success and status (Melson-Silimon et al., 2023).

Embracing the stereotype of being inherently athletic leaves many Black boys and men who are not athletic believing they are inferior and unable to achieve anything meaningful. The result is that Black boys are discouraged from exploring their potential in other areas (Melson-Silimon et al., 2023). The same is true for various professions that are not typically filled by Black men, which limits the conception among Black men and boys about where they belong in the world. Examining stereotypes depends on understanding how social identity causes individuals to embrace stereotypes specific to their membership, including racial and gender groups (Vecci & Želinský, 2019).

The individual's social identity contains a set of rules that govern group behavior (Vecci & Želinský, 2019). However, when certain characteristics are used in society to describe a specific group, the behavior of those in the group is influenced because negative stereotypes can cause negative self-views. The individuals in the group will not perform according to their best ability, often referred to as stereotype threat, evident in populations at the focus of discrimination (Vecci & Želinský, 2019). Black men are a specific racial and gender group that must cope with stereotypes in society, which often influence negative behavior. Research on negative stereotypes shows that they may cause physiological changes in the brain and body, particularly "an increased cardiovascular profile of threat and activation of brain regions used in emotion regulation, cognitive reactions, particularly to self-monitoring of performance that may be hyper-vigilant, and affective responses, such as suppressing self-doubts" (Johnson & Godsil, N. D., p. 14).

When these responses occur, the cognitive resources of Black men that could be used in performing at their actual capacity are diminished (Johnson & Godsil, N.D.). Therefore, it is crucial to discover how Black men can overcome stereotypes to ensure they perform at their best capacity in all areas of their lives and shed the cloak of the negative stereotypes that affect their behavior and outcomes. The following section will examine programs and models that exist to help Black men overcome stereotypes.

Programs and Models to Help Overcome Stereotypes

A study was conducted among Black men using a Manhood Development Program (MDP), and classes were given in the Oakland Unified School District that developed the Office of African Male Achievement (Givens et al., 2016). The MDP was formulated to assist in cultivating healthy identities among Black males to improve their achievement. The program was conducted in several schools in the district. The interventions in the study included instructors working to disassemble the stereotypes of Black men as being unemotional and hard, and to address the problem that anger is generally the only emotion expressed. The study used role modeling to assist Black males in learning how to acknowledge and express their emotions in a healthy manner.

The conversation was led by Brother Phil, who revealed how he, as a Black man, and others,

"often employ a 'cool pose' to avoid the experience of vulnerability. While he's critical of this practice, which is perceived to be the masculine way of dealing with anger, he acknowledged that he, too, as a Black man, is guilty of it at times" (Givens et al., 2016, p. 174).

Role modeling helps Black men and boys understand that they are more than what stereotypes say about them, as they interact with Black men who have overcome those depictions in their lives and professions. The study also noted that one aspect crucial to resisting stereotypes involved emotional sharing among the Black males in the study, which was recognized as a vital aspect of Black male masculinity (Givens et al., 2016).

The study acknowledged that relationships are essential to removing stereotypes in the lives of Black men as they engage with women, their children, and one another. Instructors in the study served as role models for the Black males in how they interacted with their children and others by sharing stories. The instructors pushed hard against gender norms in the family by cooking something to bring to the class or holding a baby as they talked to the class. One of the instructors, Brother Jay, emphasized how it is okay for a Black man to cook and explained how he often cooks for his family. Overall, the program instructors worked to destabilize the dominant ideas of Black manhood and serve as role models to help the participants develop a new identity of being a Black man (Givens et al., 2016).

This example demonstrates how 'showing' Black men rather than merely 'telling' them makes a longer-lasting impression.

The instructors also used popular hip-hop songs, questioned the lyrics, and worked to help the participants see that sexism, discrimination, prejudice, and stereotyping of women were contained in the songs (Givens et al., 2016). One of the most critical aspects of the intervention in the MDP program was the emphasis on relationships with other Black men. The instructors helped the participants understand that their connections with other Black men were an essential part of overcoming stereotypes. The instructors expressed caring for the participants, leading them to realize that expressing love for one another is vital.

Finally, the MDP program emphasized the need to reimagine the identity of Black males by understanding the essential contributions they can make to society. This was achieved by highlighting historical Black figures and the achievements of Black males who have made significant contributions to the world around them (Givens et al., 2016). The presentation of the historical Black figures assisted in presenting role models to the participants, which provided them with real-life examples of how Black men have overcome and realized success despite the existing stereotypes.

The participants in the MDP program revealed that they felt empowered hearing about Black men who had achieved and accomplished something important. Guest speakers from the community were brought into the program, allowing participants to hear from businessmen, community activists, and artists who helped by presenting role models and overturning the stereotypes Black men often embrace rather than seek to overcome (Givens et al., 2016). The MDP program is one example of how schools and communities can assist Black men in realizing they are in a position of power in their own lives to overcome the stereotypes that are present in society. Finally, the study emphasized the value of teachers and others in the community working to role model Black male identities to support the younger generation of Black males to see past the stereotypes and self-direct their lives (Givens et al., 2016). The community is essential in building a narrative among Black men that goes entirely against the existing stereotypes to introduce the possibilities of what Black men can achieve.

Another initiative successfully assisting Black men and boys is the Young Men, Masculinities, and Mental Health (YBMen) project (Watkins, 2019). The YBMen project began in 2008 and was a six-week social support and mental health education intervention that provided age- and gender-specific support that was culturally sensitive to educate Black men and boys about the vital nature of social support and transforming how manhood is defined. The project encouraged community-building among those participating and helped Black men and boys to challenge the rigidity of gender roles. Part of the program focused on coping and well-being to help move Black men and boys into more social interaction and support activities. After participating in the program evaluation, measures were taken to examine the project's impact, process, and outcome factors (Watkins, 2019). The project assisted Black men and boys in treating their masculinity as adaptive and functional, supporting productivity in difficult life conditions. The psychoeducational intervention was successful because it took an intersectional approach to addressing Black men and boys' socially constructed identity (Watkins, 2019). Considering how gender, race, and other factors intersect to affect Black men is crucial for any intervention.

Social interaction among Black men is vital. Research has indicated that Black men often fail to take the time to pursue activities that give them pleasure and empowerment (Jacob et al., 2023). Empowerment is crucial in the lives of Black men, and involvement in positive social change not only empowers Black men but also helps them develop self-affirmation and agency. Counseling services can also help Black men find purpose in their lives, provide positive affirmation, and help them develop "a coping strategy that affirms their intrinsic worth and beauty" (Jacob et al., 2023, p. 409). In the absence of social support networks, counseling can assist Black men in developing proactive coping mechanisms and, in a transformative process, help them reframe their experience with racism (Jacob et al., 2023). In the absence of positive coping strategies for Black men, harmful coping mechanisms may include avoidance, self-blame, or substance abuse (Jacob et al., 2023). The most positive coping strategies include active strategies centered on problem-solving, participating in a social network that supports collective problem-solving and coping, and spiritually-centered coping (Jacobs et al., 2023).

In other words, Black men can realize self-affirmation in the social context, whether it involves groups focused on hobbies, sports, or other activities that provide empowerment. Black men can realize self-affirmation in the spiritual/religious setting in their relationships with other Black men as they focus on God and spiritual matters. Black men can also realize self-affirmation in their activities within the community as they support and advocate for change in the agencies and institutions characterized by systemic racism that drives stereotypes of Black men. Black men can overcome stereotypes by boldly stepping out into their lives in their community, society, and the world around them to become change-makers as they engage in activities and initiatives in the community.

One model used to promote resilience and healing in the Black community is the Black Love, Activism, and Community (BLAC) model (Turner et al., 2022). The BLAC model is constructed on empirical research and provides a conceptual model based on loving and caring relationships, love of the Black culture and its people, and love for God, acknowledging that God loves individuals. The principles of the model include harmony, balance, communalism, authenticity, caring and compassion, self-determination, and interconnectedness. The model emphasizes "living from a foundation of spiritually infused interconnected humanity" and the principle that "a person's humanity cannot be fully realized outside of communal connection which centers spirituality not as an individualized experience, but a relational and communal one" (Turner et al., 2022, p. 552).

Although this model is used for activism, it could also be used within the Black community and among Black men and boys to build connections that assist them in supporting one another and building a foundation to assist in creating the needed resilience to overcome the stereotypes they face in society and their minds (Cozart, 2016). The spiritually centered aspect of the model supports Black men in acknowledging who they are according to God and focusing on building resilience that is spiritually based. The BLAC model can be used and adapted by community organizations and within Black churches. Building spiritually grounded relationships among Black men enables relationships such as mentor-mentee relationships, wherein older Black men who have overcome the stereotypes in their lives and risen above the societal views of Black men can serve as mentors and role models for younger Black men (Cozart, 2016).

Mentoring involves an intentional and formal relationship that helps individuals adjust and develop their identity constructively and purposefully, particularly when social systems and group experiences clash (Cozart, 2016). Mentor-mentee relationships involve a relationship in which the more experienced mentor transfers insight, wisdom, experiences, confidence, and information to the mentee in a lifelong relationship that assists the mentee in realizing their potential. The development of trust in the mentor-mentee relationship supports the ability to examine the mentee's problems, weaknesses, and questions. The relationship involves trust-building so that the mentor and mentee communication reaches beyond the surface level (Cozart, 2016). The following section will examine biblical models of mentorship and role modeling.

Biblical Models of Mentorship and Role-Modeling

The biblical text depicts mentoring examples (Cozart, 2016). For example, Moses mentored and trained Joshua, who would take his place in leading the Israelites into the promised land. The relationship between Moses and Joshua involved mentoring, and Joshua displayed the effectiveness of the mentoring he received from Moses by reminding the Israelites that they would follow Moses' commands. Another example of mentoring is depicted in the Bible as Jesus leading His disciples and spending time with them. One aspect of the mentoring relationship is observed in John 13, when Jesus set an example of what serving means, and He washed the disciples' feet. Jesus said that after doing so, He had set an example for them to serve others. The teaching moments Jesus gave the disciples were during daily living, where He corrected them, provided encouragement, and called them to step out with faith in their obedience to God (Cozart, 2016).

A study was conducted among Black males in a predominantly White university setting that involved twelve Black male students who had relationships with mentors (Cozart, 2016). The study sought to understand the impact and benefits of mentor-mentee relationships. The mentoring relationships were based on spirituality and found that the mentoring program helped Black males make more positive decisions and provided them with accountability. Involvement in the relationships with mentors also assisted the participants in understanding what God intended them to do with their lives. The mentoring relationships were found to assist in shaping the participants' character and identity and to provide them with the needed confidence to step out of their comfort zone. The mentoring relationships increased the integrity of the participants and provided them with a robust support system to help them remove themselves from negative influences (Cozart, 2016).

Small groups were held among the participants, and they revealed that these groups allowed them to ask hard questions in a non-judgmental environment, which grew their faith in God and provided a non-threatening environment for self-development (Cozart, 2016). The participants also reported the positive outcome of building healthy relationships with students of other races. Finally, the participants revealed that the mentoring program and relationships had assisted them in embracing those of different cultures and ethnicities because they had gained security in their ethnicity and identity. The mentoring relationships helped the participants grow spiritually and played a critical role in that spiritual growth. These relationships ultimately assisted the participants in engaging more in their academics. Such guidance focuses on helping the mentees understand what they can accomplish and changing their self-perceptions (Cozart, 2016).

Black churches play a central role in the Black community, uniquely situating them to assist Black men in developing a healthy identity and rising above the stereotypes and realize their potential. Within the spiritual and religious sphere, Black men who are believers in Christ Jesus can focus on what God says about them, which is much more vital than the stereotypes the world would assign to them.

Developing an identity in Jesus Christ means following the principles set out in the Bible, many of which may go against the grain of the African American culture, particularly among many of today's Black men who see themselves as only worthy if they have a lot of money and are seen as a womanizer. However, escaping stereotypes depends on taking actions that align with moral principles. Greelee (2013), in his work *'Living Out an In Christ Identity: Research and Reflections Related to Muslims Who Have Come to Faith in Jesus Christ,'* explains how developing an identity 'In Christ' involves changing the negative patterns of behavior as the person identifies more closely with Jesus than with the world.

The biggest challenge that many Black men have is knowing who they are apart from the culture and stereotypes they are accustomed to while understanding that identity can be restructured according to God's Word, freeing them from the stereotypes that have plagued their lives by changing their behavior (Greenlee, 2013). Three layers of identity exist, including the core identity, social identity, and collective identity. These layers of identity must be merged to create a positive identity that aligns with spiritual principles, supporting Black men to feel empowered and confident in who they are according to what God says they are (Greenlee, 2013). In other words, Black men must decide to live in a way that does not in any way align with the stereotypes and, having done so, free themselves from their influence over their minds and their lives. Changing the focus from what society says about them to what God says about them can assist Black men in overcoming the power that stereotypes have on their lives.

Summary

In summary, overcoming stereotypes among Black men takes a focused effort to free their minds from how they are portrayed in society. Today's Black music artists focus on money, drugs, women, and living the gangster life. Societal expectations and depictions of Black men are often negative and characterize Black men by the stereotypes that have been deeply ingrained into society. Without the needed support within the Black community and the lives of Black men, there is a tendency to embrace those stereotypes rather than seek to overcome and move past them with a healthy identity. However, more experienced Black men who have broken free of those stereotypes can serve as mentors and role models in Black communities to assist younger Black men in developing healthy identities and moving toward who God created them to be—free of the bondage of those stereotypes. Central to helping Black men overcome stereotypes are Black churches that are influential in Black communities and have the power to institute change by reaching out to the community with programs to assist Black men in achieving self-determination about who they want to be in the world.

Various programs and models that would be successful have been introduced, and the framework has been provided to construct successful programs to help Black men overcome stereotypes. However, developing an identity in God and focusing on who God says Black men are is crucial to overcoming stereotypes and developing healthy identities among Black men. Community-building will assist Black men in collectively challenging the stereotypes and their mindset about how they respond to those stereotypes and overcome them. The following chapter presents an examination of mental health issues that are prevalent among Black men, such as anxiety, depression, and posttraumatic stress disorder (PTSD), and will highlight the importance of mental health awareness and access to resources.

Chapter Four

Mental Health and Wellness

This chapter will examine the mental health issues that are prevalent among Black men, including depression, anxiety, and post-traumatic stress disorder (PTSD), barriers to mental healthcare access, and the importance of awareness and access to mental health resources. As revealed in the previous chapters, Black men cope with serious life issues, including stigma, stereotypes, racism, and historical trauma. Black men also cope with societal expectations about who they are and struggle to remain resilient with all the life stressors they experience. All these factors increase the potential for Black men to develop mental health issues. The following section will examine the mental health issues prevalently experienced by Black men.

Black Men and Prevalent Mental Health Issues

Black men experience many mental health issues noted as the number one cause of Black men's mortality and morbidity (Joseph et al., 2024). Black men are at a high risk for developing depression and post-traumatic stress disorder (PTSD) (Jones et al., 2022). Post-traumatic stress disorder is a mental health disorder that is quite common but also disabling. The prevalence of PTSD is higher among African Americans and is linked to an increased risk for hypertension, heart disease, stroke, and diabetes. Post-traumatic stress disorder may co-occur with other mental health disorders, such as major depressive disorder or substance use disorder, contributing to chronic disease and poor health outcomes. The older the individual, the greater the risk for post-traumatic stress disorder, and in Black individuals, that risk increases with age. However, post-traumatic stress disorder develops during the young adulthood of Black men, and it is held that discrimination increases the potential for the individual to develop PTSD, negatively affecting their social outcomes (Jones et al., 2022).

An additional factor in the lives of Black men that impacts them, causing post-traumatic stress disorder, is exposure to violence (Ugwuede, 2023). Living in urban, low-income areas increases the potential for Black men to be exposed to chronic violence, resulting in PTSD because they tend to mask their trauma rather than seek help. It is crucial to understand how Black men express PTSD in order it to be recognized and treated (Ugwuede, 2023). The National Center for PTSD (2020) revealed that there are considerable disparities in individuals with PTSD, and racial minority groups are at an increased risk due to the operational and regulatory processes that result in those populations encountering discrimination, stereotypes, and biases. The inability to afford insurance coverage among racial minorities affects their ability to access needed care (National Center for PTSD, 2020). Mental healthcare is an area where Black men are particularly vulnerable to stereotypes and biases that operate across society. Moreover, "there are numerous institutional and provider decision points in health care pathways that are vulnerable to the effects of bias" (National Center for PTSD, 2020, p. 2). For example, Black men may delay seeking mental healthcare treatment due to the existing biases and structural racism. Yet, delays in treatment result in worse clinical outcomes, particularly for PTSD (National Center for PTSD, 2020).

There are severe issues in the lives of Black men, in addition to trauma, racism, and stigma, which influence their trajectory toward mental health disorders. Many young Black males have fathers in prison, and the result is adverse socioeconomic outcomes. Research indicates that mental health issues may begin early in life for Black males due to the mass incarceration of Black men (Lewis & Hong, 2020). More than one million Black men are imprisoned each year, creating significant issues for their families (Lewis & Hong, 2020). Removing fathers from homes disrupts the family and weakens the community's social networks. The outcome is that young Black males do not have role models in the home, and research indicates that Black children are more than seven times more likely to have a parent imprisoned than White children (Lewis & Hong, 2020).

Black men who are imprisoned lose their sense of identity and experience psychological pain due to the loss of autonomy and liberty and changes in their self-perceptions as fathers and men (Lewis & Hong, 2020). The systemic racism of the criminal justice system has altered the identities of Black men, and once they return home, they fail to function with their families and community in a healthy manner. Incarceration has been noted in the research to result in a reduction in engagement between Black men and their children because it may erode their social skills and further reinforce stereotypes of masculinity that are unhealthy (Lewis & Hong, 2020). Unfortunately, far too many Black men experience incarceration and the resulting psychological issues that arise, increasing a long-term impact on self-perception and identity (Lewis & Hong, 2020). Once they return to their families and communities, Black men who have been incarcerated may fail to seek help for mental health issues, which disrupts the homes and communities as those men fail to function effectively.

However, mental health issues may also begin early in life for Black males due to broken families for reasons other than incarceration, which is a problem that is associated with the breakdown of the family. Research indicates that relationship stressors are more significant among Black couples, including marital abuse and child and marital-related stressors, which are linked to poorer mental health outcomes (Priest et al., 2020). Psychological responses to stress are mitigated when family relationships are emotionally close and supportive. However, when breakdowns occur in the family unit due to the issues already mentioned and others, the psychological response to stress is enhanced, and mental health issues become a problematic issue in the lives of Black men. Therefore, the family structure serves as a protective factor against mental health problems, even in the face of discrimination and racism (Priest et al., 2020). The following section will describe the barriers to seeking help for mental health disorders experienced by Black men.

Barriers to Access

The stigma associated with mental illness bars many Black men from seeking and engaging with mental healthcare, despite their experiences with anxiety, depression, or PTSD (Pederson et al., 2022). The stigma referred to is that concerning the "negative attitudes and beliefs one may hold toward mental illness and is based on a desire for social distance or separation from people who are part of the stigmatized group" (Pederson et al., 2022, p. 3). The stigma associated with mental health disorders increases the likelihood that an individual will refrain from seeking help for any disorders they may experience. Many cultural groups have not acculturated to mainstream society's beliefs and values (Pederson et al., 2022). Achieving acculturation involves a psychological process, but many groups, including African Americans, may experience acculturative discordance when it comes to seeking help for psychological distress (Pederson et al., 2022).

Additionally, a factor that affects help-seeking behavior among Black men is their propensity to turn to religion and spirituality, which is a preferred mental health disorder coping mechanism (Ward et al., 2014). Research has shown that Black men are more likely than other racial minorities to turn to religion to cope with mental health issues, which may include a relationship with God and prayer (Ward et al., 2014).

One study examined the predictors of mental health treatment-seeking among Black men and noted that predictors might include their attitudes about seeking help, the stigma associated with mental health, service affordability, constraints in the environment, and distress symptoms (Turner et al., 2024). Research shows that Black men who do access mental healthcare services "are more likely to receive services under emergency, mandated, or coerced conditions rather than voluntary conditions" (Turner et al., 2024, p. 385). Black men often fail to seek treatment due to fear and negative attitudes. However, the expectations that Black men have toward treatment may serve to inform their help-seeking behaviors or their failure to seek help.

The study examined the perceptions of Black men about the use of mental healthcare services. Seventy-six participants in the study, between 19 and 54 years, were housed in a correctional facility. Educational attainment among the men ranged from a GED to a bachelor's degree, and incarceration reasons varied from non-violent crimes to substance abuse-related crimes and harsher crimes (Turner et al., 2024).

The participants in the study revealed that they were likely to seek out mental healthcare services because there were fewer barriers in the correctional facility setting compared to seeking outpatient treatment (Turner et al., 2024). Among the participants who had experienced mental health disorders prior to incarceration, they reported problems with access. The study found that the ability to access care was a significant predictor of non-help-seeking behaviors among Black men, but fears about therapy played no role in help-seeking behaviors. The findings of the study indicate that if other barriers to help-seeking are removed, Black men are open to seeking mental healthcare services (Turner et al., 2024).

Although not explicitly stated in the study, it appears that help-seeking behaviors are less stigmatized among Black men who are incarcerated. They are less likely to be influenced by family and friends, which may hold pessimistic attitudes about seeking help for mental health symptoms, combined with reduced stigma. However, as previously noted, once Black men return to their homes, community, and society, the barriers to help-seeking behaviors persist.

Importance of Awareness and Access to Mental Health Resources

Black men are noted to be one of the largest underserved populations when it comes to mental health services (Holden et al., 2012). It is problematic that many Black men have co-occurring mental health and substance abuse disorders. The sociocultural factors and psychosocial factors that impact the help-seeking behaviors of Black men have profound implications, mainly when co-occurring disorders are present. Black men may develop various forms of mental disorders, including panic, anxiety, obsessive-compulsive, stress, and antisocial personality disorders. Policymakers and clinicians need to target those groups for treatment.

There are many problems in reaching Black men to increase awareness of the availability of services. Three areas impact the willingness of Black men to seek mental healthcare services: masculine norms, attitudes toward help-seeking, and self-stigma. Additionally, the historically shared ideas of self-reliance and strength may cause men to fail to access services (Holden et al., 2012).

The need to increase awareness of mental health among Black males and ensure they can access care is highlighted by the statistic that approximately 80 percent of all suicides occur among young Black males (Lindsey & Marcell, 2012). The health belief and socio-behavioral health models provide frameworks to help understand the factors that may influence healthcare use among Black men. Those theories indicate that factors at the individual level affect their use of health services, such as their health-related needs and personal beliefs and knowledge. Additionally, factors at the health system level affect their use of health services, including service accessibility.

A study was conducted to examine the factors that influence help-seeking for mental health problems among Black men in an urban community. The men were recruited from four organizations in a city in the Northeastern United States. Focus group discussions were conducted with the 27 participants, who had an average age of 20.4 years.

The qualitative study identified themes in the participants' statements during the focus group discussion. They expressed a belief in taking care of themselves and telling no one about their mental health issues due to their perceptions of what it means to be a man. One participant revealed, "I keep it to myself and try to work it out, figure a way to get out of the problem, whatever the problem may be, and move on with it" (Lindsey & Marcell, 2012, p. 357).

Personality factors such as pride and ego stood in the way of help-seeking, although confidence and self-assurance facilitated help-seeking (Lindsey & Marcell, 2012). The study also identified a theme of how participants described the importance of hobbies or doing something they liked to deal with mental health issues.

The participants revealed that, often, if they knew something was wrong with them emotionally or mentally, they would use spirituality. For example, one participant revealed, "If something going wrong with me and I don't know what to do about it. I'm going to Jesus first before I go to anybody, I tell you, I'm hittin' that Bible" (Lindsey & Marcell, 2012, p. 357).

One participant noted, “There’s not too many people you can talk to out here about your problems. You gotta deal with it yourself” (Lindsey & Marcell, 2012, p. 357).

Concerning the idea of seeking help for emotional and mental problems, the participants said it depended on the type of problem they were experiencing and the quality associated with the sources of help. Many participants mentioned talking to their parents, grandparents, other family members, friends, and community members. One participant stated,

“New age Blacks will talk to a psychiatrist or a therapist. But Blacks in the inner city – to them, it’s not being a man talking to somebody, a doctor…’ Cause it comes back in the older period. They didn’t have a lot of help for Blacks at that time, so it wasn’t pushed through as much. It’s not caught up as much with the new-age Black man. They went through college, and they know this knowledge, and they have the Internet so they can read up on it, and they know they have to go for the mental thing. But as for the inner city, they don’t have as much knowledge as somebody that goes to higher education. So then they don’t feel as strong because a lot of them scared, so they not gonna talk to somebody" (Lindsey & Marcell, 2012, p. 358).

The statements of the participants in the study highlighted the need to address commonly held beliefs among Black men about seeking help for mental health disorders and how, in the absence of that help, they attempt to cope with the problems in isolation (Lindsey & Marcell, 2012). Trust issues play a prominent role in the failure of Black men to seek professional help for mental health disorders because they do not feel comfortable with self-disclosure (Lindsey & Marcell, 2012).

However, there are organizations in Black communities that can play a vital role in increasing awareness of the need for, and the acceptability of, mental health services among Black men. Many Black men turn to religion and spirituality to cope with mental health disorders, which puts the Black church in a unique position to promote help-seeking behaviors (Robinson et al., 2018). Research shows that "being Black in America" harms the mental health of Black individuals (Robinson et al., 2018, p. 1097). However, the *Diagnostic and Statistical Manual of Mental Disorders* (DSM-IV) has recognized the relevance of cultural and religious sensitivity, and research has shown that prayer is an essential mechanism that can be used to relieve stress. The Black church is a vital aspect of the Black community, first established in the mid-1700s, and "as such the Black Church is in a strategic position to attract Black men and younger members and to be useful in ameliorating a plethora of social problems and conditions that plague the African American Community" (Robinson et al., 2018, p. 1098).

Research indicates that more than 90 percent of Black individuals attend church weekly, report that religion is essential in their lives, and believe in God (Robinson et al., 2018). Of those who attend church weekly, nearly 40 percent are Black males. The Black Church has the potential to increase awareness among Black men about the acceptability and need to seek mental healthcare services due to the pivotal role it plays in the lives of those men. However, the focus on Black male mental health within the Black church must be more than just providing education and holding events to promote health. What is required is a dialogue that confronts the stressors of Black men concerning masculinity, and racism, societal factors and stressors (Robinson et al., 2018).

According to Robinson et al. (2018), the Body, Mind, Spirit, Environment, Social, Transcendent Health (BMSEST) theoretical framework and the Health, Illness, Men and Masculinities (HIMM) theoretical framework may help the Black Church serve as a support network that is effective for the healthy mental health of Black men. The BMSEST theoretical framework supports a holistic perspective of religion, spirit, and health and is grounded in Maslow's self-actualization theory. The HIMM assists Black churches in their promotion of mental health among Black males because it addresses health disparities and acknowledges masculinity as a health determinant. There is a church in almost every neighborhood in the United States, especially in urban African American communities, and because it serves as the pillar of a Black community, the church is particularly suited to provide information and resources that are focused on mental health to assist in conducting outreach to Black men in the community and to increase awareness. Pastors within the Black church are the ones most likely to counsel church members, so increasing mental health literacy among pastors is essential to assist them in making referrals and encouraging congregants to seek mental healthcare services when needed (Robinson et al., 2018).

Black men are more likely to view mental healthcare services in a more positive light when the pastor of their church or the pastor of the local church advocates for help-seeking (Robinson et al., 2018). Moreover, when pastors of Black churches possess mental health literacy, they are more likely to identify church members who would benefit from mental healthcare services. Pastors and others in the church who are mental health literate can help spread awareness in the Black community by partnering with other organizations to increase awareness of the acceptability and need for mental healthcare services among Black men. Raising awareness among Black men will require a coordinated effort by the Black church in partnership with other community organizations to create a more positive narrative about help-seeking (Robinson et al., 2018).

One such program was presented in a study published in the *BMC Psychiatry Journal*, which involved a 24-week community program (Joseph et al., 2024). The program was known as the Black Impact community-based participatory research program that enrolled Black men during an annual community event. Although the study was focused on improving cardiovascular health among Black men, during week eight of the intervention, health coach sessions involved discussions surrounding stress, historical trauma, and mental health. The health coaches provided mental health strategies, resources, and information on stress management delivered by a local mental health counselor. The program included a session titled *Barbershop Talk: Real Men, Real Talk*, which emphasized the importance of Black men discussing mental health issues (Joseph et al., 2024). These types of interventions in the community hold real promise to create a dialogue around mental health among Black men and provide information that supports their help-seeking behaviors.

Community organizations, mental health providers, churches, and other stakeholders in predominantly Black communities need to partner to build awareness and increase access for Black men with mental health disorders. One such partnership was created in the state of North Carolina in an initiative referred to as the Triad Pastors Network (TPN), which worked with the North Carolina Maya Angelou Center for Health Equity (MACHE) (Gwathmey et al., 2024). The initiative sought to address the problems with health disparities among the African American population by increasing awareness and trust among Black individuals in the communities involved. Although the initiative was focused on physical health, the same method can be easily adapted to focus on mental health disorders. Each church, its pastor, and leaders attended a session that explained the initiative's focus (Gwathmey et al., 2024).

One of the TPN members had 50 churches in his district, enabling him to disseminate the information widely across several regions (Gwathmey et al., 2024). Pastors completed surveys identifying the top priorities that needed to be addressed, and an approach was established to promote and implement health ministries within the churches. Through the partnership, pastors could work in a culturally appropriate way to provide the information to the members of the communities in which their churches were situated and assist members in accessing the needed healthcare provisions. The involvement of pastors in the initiative was vital since all "faith communities are not homogenous groups of people," and the churches involved were varied in their form of worship (traditional, contemporary), so the health approaches were adapted to each specific group (Gwathmey et al., 2024, p. 564). MACHE provided health resources combined with the support of partners in the churches and community to ensure sustainability, assisting the African American communities in leveraging the assets and resources needed to make the program an ongoing offering. The approach was based on the core principle of community engagement, and through building partnerships, approaches could be tailored to reach the maximum number of individuals possible (Gwathmey et al., 2024). The approach used in this initiative provides an excellent model for community organizations, health organizations, and churches in Black communities to reach Black men, increase awareness about mental health, and ensure they can access the services needed.

Summary

This chapter examined the prevalent mental health disorders among Black men, the barriers to mental healthcare access, and the importance of awareness and access to mental health resources. Black men have high levels of anxiety, depression disorders, and PTSD due to many factors in their lives they cope with, such as racism, discrimination, poverty, and violence. The views held by Black men regarding what constitutes Black male masculinity, the stigma associated with seeking help, and the commonly and traditionally held beliefs among the Black population about mental healthcare services all work to present barriers to help-seeking behaviors. It is problematic that Black men are one of the largest underserved populations for mental health services, especially since substance abuse and mental health often present as co-occurring conditions, which increases the mental health disorders they experience.

However, this chapter has presented several programs and models that can be effectively used or adapted among Black churches, community organizations, and mental healthcare providers to reach

Black men, increase their awareness, and, ultimately, encourage their willingness to seek help for mental health services. Increasing trust in mental healthcare service providers is a crucial aspect of reaching Black men, making partnerships that disseminate information, build awareness, and point men toward the providers that can help them significantly.

The following chapter will examine the role of family dynamics in the lives of Black men as they fill their roles as fathers, sons, and partners and the positive narratives and challenges within the family structure.

Chapter Five

The Role of Family

This chapter explores family dynamics and the role of Black men as fathers, sons, and partners. The chapter will also examine positive narratives and challenges within family structures. It is crucial to understand how family is defined. Family is "a functional group living situation in which opportunities exist for at least economic and instrumental cooperation, informal communications, and reciprocated social and emotional obligations among family members" (Wilson, 2004, p. 1). Based on this definition, Black family dynamics will be examined in the following section. According to Mitchell (2021), "Most representations of African Americans throughout American history have downplayed bonds of affection and have purposefully avoided presenting them as defining characteristics of their families and communities" (para. 8). However, the information presented in this chapter will show that family is everything for Black individuals and within the Black culture.

Black Family Dynamics

In the lives of Black men, family plays a central and vital role by offering support and emotional resources (Cross et al., 2018). The support provided by families to Black men includes the nuclear family unit and the extended family. Research on the family support networks in Black families focuses on the exchange behavior between adult relatives, such as sharing housework, providing financial assistance, childcare, and transportation, so life's daily demands can be met. Research in this area revealed that most Black individuals reported supporting other Black family members and that networks exist between families despite geographical distribution. The family solidarity model helps to understand how families offer social support to one another (Cross et al., 2018).

However, intergenerational solidarity explains the ties within the Black family (Hwang et al., 2023). Intergenerational solidarity research has focused on the relationships between older parents and their middle-aged children, but emerging research has examined the relationships during the transition to adulthood for children and their parents. Intergenerational solidarity is a critical concept in the study of the family to understand the binding of intergenerational family relationships. The theoretical model of intergenerational solidarity is based on six critical dimensions, including (1) affection or emotional closeness, (2) association or the frequency of contact, (3) consensus on the similarity of values, (4) normative obligations of the filial, (5) functional or the exchanges of social support, and (6) structural or geographic proximity. Based on this framework, the connections between parents and their children extend far into adulthood as parents assist with caring for their grandchildren and adult children support their aging parents. The solidarity that children experience in their early lives predicts their solidarity with their parents later in life (Hwang et al., 2023).

Within Black families and "against the backdrop of historical trauma, racism, discrimination, and disparities, parents of racial-ethnic minority children endeavor to rear children with the hopes of opportunity, achievement, success, and wellness" (Smith et al., 2022, p. 212). Parents in Black families must prepare their children to cope with negative factors they will face in the world around them through a process of cultural socialization to instill in their children the cultural values and affirmation of how they belong to a heritage associated with resilience, which supports children's prosocial development (Smith et al., 2022).

Research shows that there are two very distinctive features of Black family structure, including that they are more likely than White families to live in an extended family situation, and they are more likely to be single parents (Ruggles, 1994). Although earlier research claimed that the struggles of slavery caused instability and disorganization in Black families, the opposite has been shown since the Black extended family helps them cope with the problems that Black families face. Earlier conceptualizations of the Black family essentially ignored the resilience that exists (Ruggles, 1994). Before 1940, single parents and children without parents accounted for most of the extended family living arrangements in Black families (Ruggles, 1994). Research shows that bonds are powerful among Black families and are characterized by strong interaction patterns (Briscoe, 2017). Black families, particularly those in the lower socioeconomic class, have adapted to their situation by combining kin networks with flexible family patterns wherein the family is defined "as the smallest, organized, and durable network of kin. Kin interact daily and provide for the needs of the children, ensuring their survival" (Briscoe, 2017, p. 102).

I personally know of one situation involving a Black man, born to a single mother, who was shot when he was two months old and was raised by his great-grandmother, grandmother, and three aunts, as well as with the interaction of other family members. This intergenerational solidarity is the type of family structure among Black families where they all work together to care for their members. The local church was integral to the family and worked as an extension of the family for the man. Ultimately, the man was raised with respect for others and a good work ethic, and he went on to marry and establish himself in the world, which would not have been possible for many in the same situation. Even after he married, he kept in close contact with those who had raised him, helping provide care for his elders as they aged, offering help with tasks, and providing financial support. That situation is typical for Black families who are tight-knit across generations.

One study examined the relationships of fifty Black families and revealed that the participants stated their kinship ties were robust regardless of their geographical location and that the economic and social status of kinship ties was stable (Briscoe, 2017). Even when Black individuals leave their homes to get married, the ties remain, and the expectation is that they would continue to help their kin when needed. For example, funerals among Black families involve traveling to the location where they are held, helping the family, and renewing relationships to provide a feeling of solidarity. Those functions within Black families provide life with meaning. Moreover, research has shown that three-generation households among Black families are essential in providing the social and financial assistance needed for children in their early years of marriage, and in turn, younger generations assist the older members in the same ways. Multi-generational involvement in the lives of Black boys is crucial since they have traditionally and historically had a difficult struggle. Expressly, "they have not been granted traditional masculine privilege or power. Social, cultural, and economic forces manifested in racism and oppression throughout American history have combined to keep Black men from assuming traditionally accepted masculine roles" (Briscoe, 2017, p. 111).

Black Men as Fathers, Sons, and Partners

Research has examined the experiences of Black men as fathers. One study was conducted among 132 Black men in rural communities in the Southern United States (Brown et al., 2019). The study noted that the risk of disengagement among Black men and their children in that region is exceptionally high and that many Black children are raised in a single-parent home. The study sought to understand relationships via intergenerational transmission among the participants. Therefore, the study examined the quality of the participant's relationship with their birth fathers or social fathers, meaning someone else in their life who served as a father figure. The study found that intergenerational transmission of parenting style was evident between fathers and their sons. Additionally, the participants who reported having close relationships with their fathers were likelier to do the same with their children (Brown et al., 2019).

In a separate study, Thomas (2024) explored the role of Black fathers who grew up without their fathers present. Thomas (2024) noted that the U.S. census revealed that approximately 49 percent of Black children live with a single mother. Those statistics are unfortunate since research has shown that a father's presence increases a child's academic achievement and reduces the potential for criminal behavior. However, this is not to say that there is no father figure in the lives of Black children, because many others, such as adoptive and stepfathers, play fatherhood roles with a high level of commitment to the children. A father figure in the lives of young Black men also reduces the risks associated with poverty, alcohol, and drugs. However, it should not be assumed that Black fathers in the United States are entirely disengaged from their children (Thomas, 2024)

In history, this myth developed when Black men could not access paid work during the Jim Crow Era, which legalized the degradation and racial segregation of Black Americans, resulting in their being weakened by severe socioeconomic constraints and lowering their ability to meet familial obligations (Thomas, 2024). Systemic racism that continues in the present also may bar Black men from achieving their potential and being in a position to financially support their children as they are forced into low-wage jobs because they are unable to afford a college education. Previous research has identified the factors Black men think are essential as fathers, including dedication, personal commitment, and being active and present in their child's life.

The six men in the study had an average age of 47.66 years, and interviews were conducted. The Black male participants in the study revealed that many of them had to forge a path in fatherhood because they had nothing else to draw on and did not have a role model who guided them. However, the participants revealed that they received proactive support from others and had present-day role models that helped them and shaped how they embodied their fatherhood role. The participants revealed barriers along the journey of being a Black father, such as societal and legal barriers and barriers related to their race (Thomas, 2024).

One participant in the study revealed, "Not having a father, I knew I didn't want to do that to my child. I think that was one of the biggest things (for me). I didn't want to do what was done to me" (Thomas, 2024, p. 27). The fathers in the study noted the importance of protecting their children and preparing them to function in the world. For example, one father stated,

"The presence of a father is really instrumental in (your children) knowing that protection and feeling safe, because when they do feel safe, they're able to explore the world in a way that they know they can come back home and be safe and secure. And I think that just the presence of a father in a home provides safety and security" (Thomas, 2024, p. 27).

The participants had a deep understanding of the many facets of fatherhood. One participant stated, "I truly think it comes down to what's needed at the time. Whether that's, you know, a strong father figure or... a princess teatime with your daughter. I think it's just knowing the role is needed and accomplishing it" (Thomas, 2024, p. 28). Another participant highlighted the importance of preparing their children and stated,

"I think what's important is trying to give your kids a little bit better start than you may have got... telling them how important it is to get a job. The biggest thing is how important it is to kind of have some good credit, and you know, I didn't care about good credit for a long time" (Thomas, 2024, p. 128-129).

One participant emphasized how his support network had empowered him to be a better father. Another participant emphasized how they watched other men who were fathers, and that helped them develop their personal fatherhood schema. One participant revealed how good fathers on television sitcoms had influenced his fatherhood style and helped him understand what a good father should do and be in their child's life. Communities were also noted as necessary among the participants, specifically community mentors (Thomas, 2024).

Reviewing Thomas' (2024) study helps to inform the exploration in this book because it indicates the critical nature of community support to empower Black men as fathers and in other areas of their lives. The study shows that Black men greatly desire to be good fathers by forging their own paths. Still, for far too many of them, there was no example in their own lives enabling intergenerational transmission of fathering practices. Other studies have shown that Black fathers cope with severe stress in their attempt to fulfill their role as fathers (Cooper et al., 2020). However, intergenerational coping patterns and processes assist them with functioning well despite the stress. One of the coping processes is via the church, where they can seek emotional support; however, many Black men lack the necessary resources to help them cope with stress related to racism to support their competence as fathers (Cooper et al., 2020). Cooper et al. (2020) and Thomas (2024) emphasize the importance of resources to help empower Black men as fathers.

Black men as partners have been examined in research, and although there are enormous benefits to marriage, Black marriage rates have experienced a decline. For example, 43 percent of Black men were married in 2000, but currently, only 37 percent are married (Mizelle, 2023). The cause of the decline has been linked to the generational impact of slavery, oppression, and mass incarceration. Research has shown that exclusion from access to opportunities for employment has further impacted marriage rates among Black men. Black men are cited as being six times more likely than other races to be arrested and nine times more likely to be incarcerated. However, for those Black men who are married, research has shown that their ideas and perceptions of marriage are significantly linked to their religiosity and spirituality. It is problematic that research on marriage and Black heterosexual males is lacking, which has created an enormous gap in the research (Mizelle, 2023).

Despite the dearth of research on Black men and marriage, one study did examine the commitment of Black men in relationships (Kogan et al., 2016). The study was conducted among Black males living in urban areas who had experienced caregiving that was unsupportive and harsh, often resulting in problematic emotion regulation and anger issues exacerbated by the experience of racism. The participants in the study were also from unfavorable socioeconomic circumstances to test whether those would negatively impact them in forming committed relationships. The study found that negative parenting and racism did produce anger that precluded young Black men from forming healthy relationships. The study emphasized the importance of intervention in the lives of young Black men to enhance future parenting practices by targeting racial socialization and increasing their ability to develop positive coping skills to deal with stressors (Kogan et al., 2016). Community support must undoubtedly be available to assist young Black men in developing the resilience they need to cope with stressors in their lives, such as racism, hostile parenting, and socioeconomic conditions, so they can establish healthy resilience and do better than their parents.

Research has shown that Black men in committed marriages have better outcomes in many areas than those who are not married (Hurt, 2013). One study examined the positive meaning that Black men derive in marriage. The study conducted interviews with 52 Black men. It was noted that men with stable employment who earn a living wage are more likely to be interested in marriage and more attractive to women. However, with the underemployment of Black men, many are not able to think about marriage. Additionally, Black men who enter college or the military are more likely to delay marriage. The study was called the "Pathways to Marriage," and participants had previously participated in the Program for Strong African American Marriages (ProSAMM) (Hurt, 2013).

The majority of the participants, who were all married, revealed that their parents had stayed together for many years, and they were raised by both their mother and father (Hurt, 2013). However, 23 % of the participants had been raised in a single-parent home by their mothers or grandmothers. Following the interviews with the participants, several areas were identified that characterize the meaning of marriage to the men, including that it provides them with secure emotional support. One participant noted,

"A friendship, meaning my wife is a person who I can sit down and talk with and would come to me and talk about things, and we know it's between us. It's not going to be something that's going to be gossiped around town" (Hurt, 2013, p. 9).

The participants also talked about how marriage is a lifelong commitment that enhances their success, anchors them, and contributes to better life outcomes. Marriage was also cited as developing a secure attachment for the participants, and it was noted that their spiritual and religious faith played a role in their marriage and commitment. One participant stated, "Marriage to me is a unification of two hearts, souls, and minds that interact for one central purpose, that is, to serve, to provide, to help, to heal, and to nurture each other" (Hurt, 2013, p.

11). Marital interventions that focus on building a marriage based on faith, commitment, and resilience could assist Black men in their marriages and help them sustain relationships.

As already stated, many Black fathers do not live in their homes with their children. Interventions have been conducted to assist those fathers in parenting their children. One study reported using a community-level approach that engaged community members in a Father's Advisory Council (FAC) to develop an intervention that would assist fathers in overcoming the barriers to involvement in their children's lives (Julion et al., 2012). The program targeted fathers with children between two and five years of age who committed to participating in the meetings. Men were recruited for the program using flyers at several daycare centers and five community-based social services programs. The intervention program was developed, and thirteen focus group meetings were held. The Council developed the program's content and videos, which were determined to be more engaging for the participants. It was determined that each session should last approximately two hours and nine weeks (Julion et al., 2012).

The program was named "Building Bridges to Fatherhood" and focused on building the knowledge and confidence of fathers, building communication between the fathers and the other parent, and parenting with a focus on guiding and nurturing young children (Julion et al., 2012). The program was developed by focusing on the participants' statements in the focus group sessions and the help that fathers need to be good fathers. Handouts and practice assignments were designed for the fathers participating in the program. The participants in the program development assisted the facilitators in learning more about how to handle their situation. One participant revealed,

"Coming to this group is one of the most therapeutic things I could have done. There are times when I thought I couldn't bear going what I am going through with my child's mothers. At times I wanted to give up, and coming to the FAC meetings gave me support and motivation and a reason why not to give up" (Julion et al., 2012, p. 10).

Another participant, who was a divorced father, revealed,

"I can't talk to my family members. I can't talk to my brothers (siblings). So for men to have this form of an outlet is real therapeutic. This support group, if you will, is superb for guys like us" (Julion et al., 2012, p. 10).

The study concluded that the formation of group-based formats assisted Black men in developing knowledge and skills to be better fathers and proved to be exceptionally robust in the community setting (Julion et al., 2012).

Another program developed to assist Black families was the "Protecting Strong African American Families" (ProSAFF) (Barton et al., 2018). The program was formulated to address the needs of two-parent Black families in the Southern United States to promote well-being in relationships and strengthen and stabilize these relationships. The program was developed based on cognitive-behavioral therapy (CBT) and social learning theory approaches and aimed to provide behavioral rehearsal, skills training, feedback, and reinforcement for how couples think about and interact in their relationships. The primary feature of the program was the attention to the experience of Black couples with contextual stressors, such as racism, finances, work, and extended families. The program was designed to assist families and couples in developing a team orientation so that relationship quality did not decline due to the stressors experienced. ProSAFF involves six sessions, one per week for two hours each and two additional sessions. Video instruction is used in the program, along with structured activities, modeling, and discussions. The most notable outcome of the program was how it boosted communication between couples, resulting in better family and couple functioning (Barton et al., 2018).

Summary

This chapter has revealed Black men's struggles as fathers, sons, and partners. The families of Black men are generally characterized by multiple generations, with each generation helping the other. Black men may be raised by family members other than their parents, and in turn, they are ready to help those family members as they age. Intergenerational solidarity exists in Black families, regardless of geographical proximity, and they stay close and contribute to one another's support in many areas due to their close bonds. However, Black men struggle in their roles as fathers and partners, as many Black men are not married to the mother of their child, and severe stressors are evident in their marriages. The positive news is that there are interventions that can assist Black men in gaining knowledge and empowerment to be better fathers and marital partners. The following chapter will discuss the educational experiences of Black men, the barriers that exist, and how Black men have persevered and overcome the challenges to realize achievement and success.

Chapter Six

Educational Journeys

This chapter will discuss the educational experiences of Black men, from K-12 to higher education, the barriers to success, and stories of achievement and perseverance. It will further examine how Black men, despite systemic racism and discrimination, manage to overcome the barriers to success. Additionally, it will show that Black men benefit from mentoring throughout their educational and professional journeys.

Struggles in the Educational Setting

According to Wint et al. (2022), "educational research in the United States often ignores the resilience and strengths of Black boys and men" (p. 183). Most research has failed to examine education among Black boys in grades lower than their adolescent years; however, Wint et al. (2022) conducted a study with that specific focus.

They noted that discussions concerning education among Black boys have failed to "contextualize the complexity of their experiences over time" (Wint et al., 2022, p. 184). The study was based on the Contextualized Life Course-Intersectional Framework (CLICIF) that emphasizes the tenets of life course theory, including developmental processes, historical place and time, linked lives, timing, and human agency (Wint et al., 2022). Within this theoretical framework is a protective layer of cultural factors that support Black boys' educational success. Intersectionality theory also helps to understand the educational vulnerabilities experienced by Black boys across all developmental stages. For example, the identities of Black boys are gendered, racialized, and shaped across different historical and sociocultural contexts. One protective factor is the family's role in supporting Black boys' educational success (Watson, 2024; Wint et al., 2022). The community setting exposes Black boys to role models that affect their educational trajectory (Wint et al., 2022). For example, in many communities, college-educated and professionally successful Black men can serve as role models to young Black boys in the community. Whether they are lawyers, business professionals, successful athletes, or working a simple manual labor job and caring for their family, Black men who have risen above the negative and false conceptualizations of who they are shine a light into their community and serve as role models for what Black men can achieve despite the struggles they face.

However, it is unfortunate that as young Black boys enter preschool, they meet a system that is already prejudiced against them and more likely to place them in special education classes than children of other races. (Wint et al., 2022). Black children in preschool have been expelled at twice the rate of others, and boys are expelled at 4.5 times the rate of children of other races and genders. It is also problematic that Black boys who attend state-funded programs are more likely to be taught by teachers of different races and ethnicities, which may create racial bias, resulting in harsher disciplinary practices toward them. Teachers may also be biased concerning the competence of Black boys, and the interactions are more likely to be negative. Those negative interactions create a lack of trust in Black boys toward adults in the educational setting, putting them at a significant disadvantage. While teachers are uniquely positioned to set the stage for Black boys' success positively, that is often not what occurs (Wint et al., 2022).

However, in the preschool setting, where the way Black boys play and learn is nurtured, they are socially and emotionally prepared to enter school and gain confidence in their educational journey (Wint et al., 2022). Black boys who do not attend preschool face the same problems when they enter elementary school, and it is problematic that in the school setting, teachers often treat Black boys as older than other children and fail to support their need to be guided, nurtured, and supported. Teachers have been found in research to view Black boys as having more behavioral challenges, causing teachers to focus more on behavior than nurturing them in the educational setting. These problems have a cumulative impact as standardized testing is a challenge for many Black boys, reflective of a "cumulative effect of systemic challenges evident in many minoritized communities, such as inadequate educational resources and teaching as well as insufficient skills development and test preparation training" (Wint et al., 2022, p. 196).

As Black boys enter middle and high school, they are more likely than their peers to encounter racism and discrimination, dealing with disciplinary referrals that are unwarranted and often related to a perception of disrespect of the school's dress code (Wint et al., 2022). However, those referrals may result in suspension and expulsion, putting the boys at an increased risk of falling behind in their schoolwork and becoming alienated from their teachers and peers. These occurrences further drive distrust toward teachers among Black boys as they cope with oppression and develop a negative self-perception of their academic abilities. Furthermore, teachers in the high school setting may discourage Black boys from going to college as they are often not given the needed support to prepare for standardized exams and admissions for college. According to Wint et al. (2022), what is needed is for schools and their teachers and staff, as well as counselors, to gain awareness of the challenges experienced by Black boys and work as change agents by advocating for the boys and interacting with their families to ensure they have the opportunity to attend college. Doing so requires the development of authentic relationships with the boys, their families, and the community. If this is done, it can potentially change Black boys' educational outcomes (Wint et al., 2022).

The Importance of Mentors and Role Models in the Educational Setting

The National Mentoring Resource Center (NMRC) is an Office of Juvenile Justice and Delinquency Prevention division that describes mentoring that is school-based:

"as a flexible relationship-based interaction between school personnel, volunteers, and students that emphasizes facilitating academic gains, improving school connectedness, increasing attendance rates, personal growth, artistic expression, future planning, goal-setting, and social-emotional development" (Collins, 2022, p. 13).

The NMRC views school-based mentoring as a cost-effective method to increase positive relationships for students, supporting academic achievement and social-emotional growth (Collins, 2022).

According to Sánchez (2016), writing for the National Mentoring Resource Center, "both formal and informal mentoring have the potential to benefit Black boys in a range of areas, including academics, social-emotional well-being, mental health, and preventing risky behaviors" (p. 1). However, Black boys must have Black male mentors due to the cultural mistrust that may otherwise exist (Sánchez, 2016).

There are challenges in many cases in obtaining Black male mentors. For example, systemic racism thwarts the ability of many Black men to serve as mentors and role models for Black boys in the educational system. The problems were revealed by Bell (2019), who states that research indicates that there are too few Black men to serve as role model. However, the problem goes deeper than the lack of role models, as there are systemic practices that bar Black men from serving in roles to support Black boys. Bell (2019) recounts his work with an organization that sought to increase the number of Black men who could serve as mentors for young Black individuals. Bell (2019) held a meeting and discovered that many Black men were willing to give their talent and time to serve.

The men were from the community and had experience with the challenges and barriers they had gone on to overcome. However, there was just one problem. Approximately 80 percent of those willing to mentor in the community had previous criminal convictions, so they were disqualified from serving as mentors and role models. The organization Bell was working with would not budge on their 'standards,' and the opportunity for those men who could have made a difference in young Black students' lives and educational trajectories was lost. Bell (2019) calls for leveraging the lives of those whom society sought to destroy so the cycles of oppression could end.

The initiative of President Obama, *My Brother's Keeper* (MBK), acknowledged the need for boys of color to have mentoring (Sánchez, 2016). Mentoring in the Black community has been a significant area of focus in the United States. Mentoring assists Black boys in coping with the barriers and challenges of crucial institutions, such as schools, that affect their future. Adult Black male mentors have a positive impact on how Black boys view themselves and their educational trajectory, which is significant since research has shown that Black boys are vulnerable and tend to disengage from the academic setting.

Black male mentors also help Black boys in the educational setting by assisting them in overcoming the assumptions of teachers that they do not achieve well and that they are likely to have discipline problems (Sánchez, 2016).

Sánchez (2016) reported that one study involved a *Helping Hands* program that provided group mentoring for Black boys in third through eighth grade. The program was instituted in 26 middle and elementary schools over three years with more than 1,400 participants. The study found that math scores rose, and those involved in the mentoring program realized higher grade point averages.

In a separate study, a mentoring program involved the *Brotherhood*, an after-school program for Black boys in the high school setting. The findings showed an increase in the grade point averages for those who participated, which rose from the previous 2.43 to 2.83 over the three years of the program. Sánchez (2016) reported a third study that involved nearly 300 Black males between the ages of ten and 24 who were assigned an informal mentor. The findings revealed that among those with a mentor, there was nearly a threefold likelihood of achieving good grades (Sánchez, 2016).

How Mentoring Helps Black Men Realize Success: Breaking Down the Barriers

David Jacoby Collins, a Black male educator, revealed how a single mother raised him with only a high school diploma. Collins' household income was below the poverty line, and he lived in a crime-ridden neighborhood characterized by impoverishment (Collins, 2022).

Collins (2022) revealed the following:

"My peers, including my cousin, Carl., turned away from school and toward gang activity. The high school I attended was populated mostly by Hispanic and African American students. The teaching staff was populated with mostly White teachers. As a student, I always wanted African American mentors in school, but they were very few. As an educator, I strive to be a mentor for the African American student population, especially the boys. My aim is to give African American students hope for a prosperous future and guidance to success" (p. 9).

Collins (2022) went on to reveal the following:

"My personal experiences as an African American male student in secondary school are inescapable. I experienced being tracked into classes that were well below my ability. I experienced seeing my fellow African American male classmates drop out, get kicked out, or just get left out of academic opportunities. I remember craving academic guidance from teachers who looked like me and understood my background. I was fortunate enough to be noticed by Mr. Brown, who took special interest in my academic and personal development, but so many of my friends were not. My childhood friend repeated seventh grade two times before dropping out of school. I often saw him hanging out on the streets, looking more and more like a vagabond. I watched KJ, one of the most charismatic young men I have ever met, sit in school daily while being ignored by our teachers before he used his natural talents to start a local gang and drug business. His potential could have been and should have been recognized and refined in school. What a waste" (Collins, 2022, p. 9).

Unfortunately, this is an all-too-familiar theme in the academic setting for African American boys. From this perspective, Collins (2022) focused his Doctoral dissertation on mentoring for Black boys in the academic setting. Collins' (2022) study was conducted by recruiting ten participants; however, all but three dropped out for various reasons. The three that remained in the study participated in a *Chamber of Scholars* mentoring program. The first participant, Mark, related how he had previously not invested in his academic studies 100%. However, the mentoring program caused him to engage more fully and put forth a better effort. Mark took just four weeks of mentoring to show signs that he increasingly identified with his academics. Mark's attitude wholly changed toward his academics at week ten, and he talked about his confidence and pride concerning his academic success and growth (Collins, 2022).

The second participant, James, after ten weeks in the mentoring program, changed from feeling defeated and contributing only 50% of his effort to his academics to revealing that he enjoyed school and realized its importance and how he had made better grades and was focusing on doing even better (Collins, 2022). The third participant, Ezra, revealed that the mentoring program had changed his attitude from not mattering to teachers to his singing the praises of three teachers whom he had realized cared exceptionally. All participants reported feeling like most teachers cared about their academic progress. However, the mentoring program assisted the participants in focusing their efforts on their academic success and embracing the belief that it would make an enormous difference in their future (Collins, 2022). Collins is an example of a Black man who rose above the barriers and challenges to realize success. Moreover, Collins serves as an example of a Black man who succeeded in his life and reached back to take the hands of other Black males who needed someone to show they cared and serve as a role model.

Another example of mentoring took place in the high school setting. Ross (2022) described his mentoring relationship with a Black male student named Ben (pseudonym). When Ross met Ben, they reviewed his schedule because the student dreamed of pursuing college football. However, Ben's transcript revealed that he struggled academically, got low grades, and even failed some courses. By learning about Ben's short- and long-term goals, Ross was able to help him via mentoring in a close relationship that emphasized that Ben was cared for and that he had support in realizing success. When the school year ended, "Ben's grades were phenomenal. He earned A's and a B during his senior year. After his stellar academic performance during his senior year, he received several scholarships for *Call Me MISTER* (2019) and other minority teaching programs" (Ross, 2017, p. 4). Ben attended a college and acquired his bachelor's degree in elementary education. Ross (2017) revealed that Ben had a really negative view of school before mentoring, felt it was not for him, and wanted to drop out. Research shows that the experiences that Black male students have in school result in negative perceptions of teachers and negative perceptions of them by teachers (Ross, 2017).

Mentoring is also crucial in the college setting. According to Watson (2024), problems exist with retaining Black males in college settings. Part of the problem is the lack of Black male staff. The retention efforts at colleges and universities fail to consider Black males' views about what would be most likely to help them remain in college. To examine these issues, Watson (2024) conducted a study at a university in the Midwest. It is problematic that the factors affecting the retention of Black male students in college have not transformed over the past nearly two decades, even though there have been enormous economic, political, and social changes. One of the most significant coping strategies used by Black males in college is peer mentoring or support. Watson's (2024) study was a qualitative phenomenological study that interviewed six Black male students. Mentoring programs offered by higher education institutions (HEI) were found to be a critical support mechanism for Black males in college. Black male students who mentored other Black male students, for example, those who had been in college for more than one year, served as mentors, which was found to be a practice that assisted with the motivation to persist and succeed. The university at the focus of Watson's study received grants to target minorities and provide them with success coaches and peer mentors. When support is consistent in the university setting for Black male students, they can better create a sense of belonging, persist, and succeed in college (Watson, 2024).

Thomas E. Cummings, a successful business entrepreneur for 30 years, presented his doctoral dissertation examining the critical success factors among Black male entrepreneurs. Collins (2019) noted that "African Americans have been establishing business enterprises since the pre-Civil War era. While they continue to open businesses today, their success rate and longevity lag behind that of their White counterparts" (p. 15). The study was conducted among Black male entrepreneurs in Monroe County, New York. The participants in the study were seven Black men who owned at least 51 percent of the business and had at least a high school education, although some participants had a bachelor's or master's degree. The critical success factors for Black male entrepreneurship identified in the study included a resilient mindset, preparation for coping with systemic and direct racism, and knowledge and possession of the strategies needed to access financial capital (Cummings, 2019).

Possessing those critical factors depends on educational attainment, as well as building strong community contacts and establishing solid banking relationships to seize business opportunities (Cummings, 2019). However, one of the most valuable resources that the participants noted was the availability of mentors, especially during the early business implementation phase and to support business growth. Mentors provide valuable guidance in unfamiliar business situations, help Black male entrepreneurs with the learning curve, and support the business's longevity. One participant stated,

"I personally think it's very, very important to have mentors. Even if you don't define them as a mentor, just to have people you can bounce things off of. Especially, when you first start in business, and if you've never run a business, there are going to be so many gaps. I was very, very lucky. I had a local owner willing to give me advice and spend time with me. Any time I had a question, I could just pop over. I didn't even need an appointment. He would answer any question that I may have had" (Cummings, 2019, p. 83).

Daymond John is one excellent example of a Black male entrepreneur who realized success. Daymond John is a millionaire investor and business mogul (Smith, 2023) who started a clothing line (FUBU) in 1989 with just $40.00 while working at a restaurant. He first learned how to sew in his mother's basement (The Wharton School, 2020). In an interview with The Wharton School (2020), he expressed that he believes having a business degree is crucial, but mentors are even more critical. FUBU did not realize overnight success, but he worked hard and turned the company into a six-billion-dollar success (Smith,

2023). Daymond revealed that his success was enormously supported by the mentors he had in his life and noted that he often speaks about how important mentors are and that he is currently involved in mentoring (John, 2024).

According to Daymond, his friend and present mentor informed him that a study found that business startups with mentors can raise seven times more money and realize 3.5 times better growth (John, 2024). He revealed that his mentors ranged from his mother and stepfather to his business partners, children, and others, such as Ralph McDaniels. According to Daymond John (2024), "Being around like-minded people and mentors is the number one reason for my success" (para. 10). He related how his first mentor was a man who owned a neighborhood corner store, emphasizing how mentors are all around the individual and they should tap into the wealth of knowledge and information that is present (Daymond, 2024; The Wharton School, 2020).

Summary

The struggles experienced by Black males in the educational setting begin early in life at the preschool age, where they are viewed as having less ability and more behavioral problems. These factors follow them throughout their educational trajectory, and they feel like outsiders and fail to develop a sense of belonging in school. Black children experience disciplinary actions and expulsion at a higher rate than their White peers. Systemic racism in the educational setting creates a lack of trust for teachers among Black males, and they feel that they are not cared for, causing them to disengage from their academic studies.

However, mentoring represents an excellent method for reaching Black males and supporting their educational perseverance and success. Research shows that mentoring offers extraordinary benefits for Black males and helps them to become more engaged in their education, create resilience, and increases academic achievement and success. Mentoring is particularly essential for Black males in middle, high school, and college settings because it gives them someone to turn to for advice, to receive encouragement, and to provide direction. Unfortunately, too few Black men are available to serve as role models and mentors. However, informal mentors in the educational setting, in the form of peer mentors, are effective in helping Black males persevere and achieve in school.

Several initiatives have been presented, such as *My Brother's Keeper*, *Helping Hands*, *Community of Scholars*, and *Brotherhood*, which offer mentoring to Black boys in the educational setting, resulting in better grades. Mentoring helps Black men and boys overcome barriers to educational success. When Black men mentor Black boys in the academic setting, they apply themselves and have better outcomes. When Black male teachers mentor Black students, the students develop a better sense of self and feel valued. It also opens the door for them to develop positive relationships with other teachers who support their educational achievement.

However, it was revealed that insufficient Black staff members are available in schools. Mentoring is associated with assisting Black males to realize not only success in school but also business success. Although success is not dependent on a college degree, Daymond John believes it is preferable to realize business success. However, Daymond John and other successful Black men reveal the necessity of mentoring for success and mentoring other Black people to help them realize the same success. The information revealed in this chapter aligns with what has been written in previous chapters about the need for Black men to lift other Black men and the need for a community approach in this endeavor. Black men are uniquely positioned to understand the need for mentoring young Black men to help them find their place in the world and to help them develop a strong self-identity and self-determination.

Chapter Seven

Economic Empowerment

The systemic racism and gendered racism faced by Black men have been revealed already in this book. However, the effects that racism has on Black men in terms of their economic pursuits and empowerment have not yet been examined. The previous chapter revealed the problems that Black boys and men experience in the educational setting, which serve to contribute to their economic struggles. The focus of this chapter is economic empowerment among Black men. The economic challenges Black men face, as well as the economic opportunities that exist, will be examined. The examination will also include successful examples of Black male entrepreneurs and those who have advanced in their careers despite the challenges. First examined will be the challenges and barriers that Black men uniquely face that are not generally present in the lives of their White counterparts.

Economic Barriers and Challenges

Black men face significant barriers to achieving in the economic areas of their lives. It is problematic, according to Roque et al. (2022), that although the economy largely had recovered economically from the pandemic, the economic recovery highlighted the effects of ongoing systemic racism. Many Black men experience persistent economic and employment opportunity gaps. The unemployment rate is higher among Black men than their White peers, and they are significantly under-employed. The reality is that many more Black men are unemployed than the statistics show, "further contributing to greater poverty, reduced financial stability, and a lack of generational wealth in Black families and communities" (Roque et al., 2022, para. 8). Research shows that the problem associated with mass incarceration of Black men has resulted in a disproportionate wealth gap in Black communities across many decades (Grawert & Craigie, 2020). In 2019, income inequality was recorded at the highest rate (Grawert & Craigie, 2020). A Brennan Center report reveals that when Black men have criminal convictions, they are set up for diminished earnings across their lifespan, perpetuating poverty and driving economic inequality (Grawert & Craigie, 2020). For example, when a Black man is convicted of a misdemeanor crime, his earnings are reduced by approximately 16 percent each year (Grawert & Craigie, 2020).

When Black men are imprisoned, they lose earnings for the years they are incarcerated (Grawert & Craigie, 2020). The same is true for White men who are imprisoned, but their earnings generally recover upon release; however, that is not the case for Black men. White men who are incarcerated lose approximately $270,000.00 in lifetime earnings, but Black men lose approximately $360,000.00 (Grawert & Craigie, 2020). Black men are at a high risk of not acquiring a sound education, which can affect their labor market success following incarceration (Western & Sirois, 2018). There are also problems for Black men who are incarcerated related to stigma. When they are released, they face criminal stigma that is intensified and generally have weak network connections, making employment difficult to obtain (Western & Sirois, 2018). The stigma is not specific to having been incarcerated but is linked to the criminal record they carry with them after prison (Western & Sirois, 2018). Research shows that once having applied for a job, the callback rate is three times higher for White individuals than for Black individuals with equivalent resumes (Western & Sirois, 2018).

Hyman (2006), in a report published by the Joint Center for Political and Economic Studies, revealed that when Black men "do well economically, they are more likely to see themselves and be seen as viable marriage partners" (p. 3). Among Black men, the economic condition is seen as the reason for the decline in marriage that is disproportionate among Black individuals, evidenced by a severe decline in employment rates. Hyman (2006) believes that the reason goes beyond the things Black men control and is related to the structural changes that have occurred in the U.S. economy, coupled with higher rates of incarceration. However, education is vital to support Black men's function as citizens, partners, and fathers. Despite these protective factors, fewer men are attending college. The lack of education often leads to Black men being involved in the sale of illegal drugs, increasing their risk for incarceration (Hyman, 2006). When men leave prison, it impacts their communities as the men are less adapted to community life than prior to incarceration and have no job skills, putting them at an increased risk for reoffending (Hyman, 2006).

It has been proposed that having a criminal record works to reinforce racial stereotypes (Western & Sirois, 2018). Moreover, Black men who have been imprisoned are shown in research to have lower levels of education and work experience, as well as health problems that stand in the way of successful employment. For example, prior to arrest, Black men are more likely to have dropped out of school, been under-employed, experienced housing instability, and suffered from disease and chronic pain in addition to other life stressors. Once they are incarcerated, they return to society and face the same severe barriers. Black men often are in social isolation upon their release from prison (Western & Sirois, 2018).

Policymakers must move toward ensuring Black men are provided with real second chances by expunging old criminal records and providing opportunities for high-quality education in prisons (Grawert & Craigie, 2020). Additionally, the social safety net must be addressed, and exclusions removed for criminal conviction in public housing access and access to benefits that would support

Black men getting back on their feet after prison and thriving in society. A final recommendation is that diversion programs should be developed to deal with Black men who have committed low-level crimes to ensure they can avoid conviction while completing a diversion program and earning the right to remain in society and maintain their employment. Grawert and Craigie (2020) stated that:

"Allowing the economic consequences of a conviction or imprisonment to last a lifetime is a moral failure. For our economy to be truly built on racial and economic justice, the millions of Americans who've been through the system must be given a real second chance" (para. 16).

Black men who have been imprisoned need a social support system that is undergirded by programs in the community that have an intense focus on helping Black men with the transition from prison back into society. Such programs would help them develop a network of connections supporting their ability to become employed and reintegrate into society. Although recommendations have been made for diversion programs, and Black leaders should inevitably work closely with governmental and policy officials to institute those changes, unfortunately,

Black men are still being incarcerated at higher rates than their White counterparts. A community-based effort that involves faith leaders, churches, community organizations, and grassroots efforts to develop programs to assist Black men would go a long way in helping them overcome their criminal convictions. As the programs work with the Black men who have been incarcerated, they will become better known in the community, which will allow them to make the connections needed to obtain employment.

Even at a young age, Black males face problems that must be overcome to develop prosocial behavior that supports them in realizing success (Harris & Kruger, 2022). However, it is not possible to examine the experiences of Black males through the same lens as that of White males, making intersectionality theory vital because it looks at how the Black male experience is shaped by the systems of oppression that interlock around gender, social class, and race. A study was conducted among Black males aged 12 years and divided them into two groups that participated in focus groups. Although some participants noted that their identity was related to being intelligent, a leader, trustworthy, and powerful, other participants revealed their identity was related to being feared, targeted, scared, and discriminated against by society (Harris & Kruger, 2022).

The discrimination the participants faced was revealed to include media portrayals and segregation of Black communities (Harris & Kruger, 2022). The differences identified between the low and high prosocial participants were that participants in the low prosocial group had a more negative view of their interactions with White people, and the high prosocial group had more positive views of their interactions with White people. This study highlights the need for young Black males to have mentors to assist them in developing a strong self-identity so they can function confidently in the world around them. Specifically, there is a need to consider the developmental perspective among young Black males to assist them in coping with discrimination and racism in their developmental outcomes (Harris & Kruger, 2022). The following section will examine how support mechanisms assist Black men with economic empowerment.

Support for Economic Empowerment of Black Men

Initiatives such as the 100 Black Men of America, Inc. offer hope to empower Black men economically. The stated mission of 100 Black Men "is to improve the quality of life within our communities and enhance educational and economic opportunities for all African Americans" (p. 2). The vision of 100 Black Men is to create environments that empower Black males to gain self-sufficiency. The organization is committed to supporting economic empowerment and intellectual development among the youth, based on the principles of justice, spirituality, family, and integrity. The 100 Black Men initiative comprises members dedicated to working in a collaborative environment with community and corporate partners to deliver programs to Black youth, their communities, and families. The initiative is based on a mentoring model (100 Black Men of America, Inc., 2019).

The various aspects of the program include supporting scholars with financial provisions for college, gaining knowledge about financial services, skills development, professional development, job preparation, expanding networking opportunities, and knowledge of banking (100 Black Men of America, Inc., 2019). The initiative also provides $10,000 for each chapter located in various locations in the United States to implement a pathway-to-success program. Some chapters include those in states such as Illinois, New York, Florida, Pennsylvania, and Los Angeles, among many other locations. Scholarships are offered to students through the African American Primary Challenge program. Many universities are involved in scholarship programs with the initiative.

One of the Black males who participated in the program revealed how he grew up in a single-parent household with only his mother, and that resulted in him not having a strong male role model. However, 100 Black Men provided the necessary mentoring to help him. The participant stated,

"The 100 Black Men showed me that it wasn't anyone else's responsibility but mine to make sure my work was done before anything else. The 100 also challenged me to hold myself more accountable in time management because, in college, you have so much free time that if you're not prepared for it, you will not know what to do with it. When I arrived on campus, I was able to reconnect with some of my Beautillion brothers, which allowed me to build an even stronger relationship with them. Having someone I previously knew on campus to help me with this big transition into a completely different environment immediately put my mind at ease" (100 Black Men American, Inc., 2019, p. 26).

Programs such as 100 Black Men are needed for all Black males to prepare them long before they reach college age. One participant in the initiative noted how he had become involved in eighth grade. The participant stated explicitly:

"I have been better able to understand myself as an individual. I am thankful to the well-trusted and dedicated men who have invested countless hours into the program. Joining the program as an eighth grader was quite intimidating because I was, in fact, the youngest in the chapter. That feeling didn't last long because the mentors and older mentees present would always make me feel comfortable and worth every second of their time. I was able to craft my entrepreneurship and public speaking skills through hands-on activities, engaging presentations, and weekly practice. The 100 Black Men of America, Inc. has made me who I am today. With all of the exposure to different career fields, service-learning opportunities, and college readiness programs, I feel confident and motivated to enter college and begin manhood" (100 Black Men of America, Inc., 2019, p. 28).

The founder of Black Men of America, Inc., and entrepreneur John Hope Bryant stated that a plan for the economic empowerment of Black men should include education, financial literacy, computer education and access, role modeling and mentoring, internships and apprenticeships, and access to capital for all Black men. However, Bryant also noted that while many non-profit initiatives exist in these areas, Black men are not prioritized (Black Men of America, Inc., 2019).

The work of Black Men of America, Inc. reveals how programs and initiatives can be developed to target Black males at an early age, which is essential to help them overcome the barriers they face to economic empowerment in the future. Notably, the idea of mentors and role models is a recurring theme, highlighting its importance in supporting Black males throughout their educational trajectory and into their early careers. Young black males can garner enormous support from these initiatives and protect themselves from failing miserably in school and possibly entering a life of crime. The 100 Black Men initiative is an excellent model that can be used in Black communities and churches to support young Black males early in life so they can overcome the barriers they face to educational achievement and economic empowerment.

Successful Black Male Entrepreneurs

Byron Allen is one example of a successful Black male entrepreneur. However, he had to overcome considerable barriers to realize success. For example, Allen, a media mogul, faced challenges with racial and economic discrimination (Pantin, 2021). He sued Charter and Comcast when they refused to carry his channels. Those providers barred Allen's business, Entertainment Studios, and he sued them in court, which ultimately went to the Supreme Court but failed in his pursuit (Pantin, 2021).

Despite the struggle against racism that Allen has experienced, he has been wildly successful. Allen founded his business in the early 1990s and owns 36 stations in approximately 21 markets. He also owns *The Weather Channel* and 12 other HD networks, as well as free streaming networks such as Sports.TV and theGrio (Hosikison, 2022).

Allen began his career as a comedian, appearing on Johnny Carson's *Tonight Show* at 17 (Hosikison, 2022). Although he is the founder and CEO of Entertainment Studios, his prior business went into involuntary bankruptcy, so Allen has overcome many struggles to realize his current success (Hosikison, 2022). However, even though Allen is a billionaire, he still struggles with discrimination in the industry. For example, he filed a lawsuit against McDonalds in 2021, claiming racial discrimination because the business refused to advertise on his channels. Allen stated,

"This is about the economic inclusion of African American-owned businesses in the U.S. economy. McDonalds takes billions from African American consumers and gives almost nothing back. The biggest trade deficit in America is the trade deficit between White corporate America and Black America, and McDonald's is guilty of perpetuating this disparity. The economic exclusion must stop immediately" (Hosikison, 2022, para. 10).

Byron Allen's success story is about resilience despite the systemic racism in America. However, he did not achieve all that he has without support from others in the form of mentors. When he was young, his single mother could not afford daycare, so he was taken to work with her at NBC (Gaydos, 2021). Allen was mentored from a young age by individuals such as Johnny Carson, Bob Hope, Red Foxx, and others. Allen decided early on that television production and comedy was his purpose in the world, influenced by his mentors (Gaydos, 2021).

Another success story of a Black entrepreneur is found in David Steward, an IT entrepreneur (Young, 2024). Steward grew up in the South when it was highly segregated, and his father was a trash collector, janitor, and mechanic. He had seven siblings. However, Steward graduated from Central Missouri University and purchased his first business in the early 1980s using community bank loans. His path was not easy, and his car was repossessed because he often did not receive a paycheck in the early days of his business. However, Steward is the wealthiest African American in the United States, topping even Robert Smith, a private equity billionaire (Young, 2024).

Steward is the majority owner of the *World Wide Technology* company, having invested an initial $250,000.00 with his partner Jim Kavanaugh. According to him, the key to success is taking risks, overcoming fears, and believing in the possibilities. Moreover, Steward says that one must be willing to "put everything on the line because you know you've been called upon to do something very special" (Young, 2024, para. 6).

David Steward noted that his mentors made an enormous difference in his life and helped him realize success. He notes that his first mentor was his father (Taylor, 2024). Steward revealed that his parents struggled to provide for the family, but his father created opportunities for himself. He has committed himself to mentoring small businesses to help develop the next generation of minority businesses, building on his experience with the Boy Scouts and how he developed core values about how he leads, in his decision-making, and in working with customers. Steward invests heavily in developing and training the next generation of leaders via the Boy Scouts. Steward stated:

"I think the community we are trying to create is a better one for the next generation behind us and the generation behind them. I am honoring the people before me who put me in the best position I can be – the position I am today. I believe 'to whom much is given, much is required.' I think what is required of me is to ensure that the next generation and the generation behind them have a better quality of life, that they are standing on my shoulders and are getting the best I can give, so they can do better. I just want to be an example for them to look to as they are guiding and living their lives" (Taylor, 2024, para. 13-14).

David Steward exemplifies how he was mentored and has devoted his life to mentoring others to help them succeed.

Summary

The unemployment rate is significantly higher among Black men when compared to White men. Additionally, more Black men are incarcerated, exacerbating their problems with employment once released. Part of the problem is the lack of networks among Black men after incarceration and the stigma associated with having been imprisoned. Structural elements in the U.S. economy contribute to the problems experienced by Black men, reducing their ability to marry and negatively impacting Black communities. Lack of education is also a contributing factor that stands in the way of economic empowerment. Failure to achieve in education often puts Black males on a trajectory for criminal behavior. There is a need for policymakers to address the issue because Black men lack the social safety net required to support their economic advancement. There is also a need for Black males to receive support to assist in developing the prosocial behaviors needed to succeed in the face of discrimination.

However, initiatives such as 100 Black Men of America, Inc. provide hope to support Black men in developing connections and receiving mentoring to achieve their goals. Initiatives such as 100 Black Men also offer financial support to young Black males. Despite the challenges that Black men face regarding economic success, there are examples of successful Black male entrepreneurs such as Byron Allen and David Steward, who have overcome and continue to overcome racism and discrimination and achieve enormous success. However, both Allen and Steward note that mentors were critical to their success. There is a need for more initiatives in communities across the United States to support Black men's development, education, and economic empowerment.

Chapter Eight

Navigating the Workforce

This book, having examined many aspects of Black men's identity, including in the family, community, and educational settings, moves toward an examination of the experiences of Black men in various professional fields, including the problem of discrimination and how it is possible to build supportive networks in the workplace. The issue of discrimination is an area that most, if not all, Black men can identify within the workplace. The following section will describe the discrimination that Black men face in the workplace and the myriad forms of racism that exist. The section also highlights the need for psychological safety and cultural sensitivity in the workplace.

Discrimination of Black Men in the Workplace and the Need for Psychological Safety and Cultural Sensitivity

Racism still exists in the workplace despite the growth of diversity in the United States (Wingfield, 2014). The reality is that "disturbing patterns of racial segregation still remain" (Wingfield, 2014, p. 240). Although cultural and social changes have occurred, the workplace is still, to a large degree, racially segregated (Wingfield, 2014). There is an overrepresentation of Whites in managerial and professional roles that offer higher salaries and more opportunities for advancement, while Blacks are in lower-paid and lower-status positions and have less growth potential (Wingfield, 2014). Although Wingfield's study was reported in 2014, ten years later, not much has changed, as evidenced by a recent report stating that, although the rates at which Black men are graduating have increased enormously, Black men are still missing from among the Fortune 500. Based on graduation rates, there should be 50 Black

CEOs, but there are still just four Black men listed (Spriggs et al., 2020).

Time Warner's former CEO, in his report *'Being Black in Corporate America,* stated, "I thought the cohort that came through in the mid-90s was just the beginning, and that there'd be a lot more. It just didn't happen" (Spriggs et al., 2020, para. 8). Research has been conducted to examine the experiences of Black professionals, but the findings are discouraging. For example, even Black men from the most wealthy families face the problem of sliding into poverty (Spriggs et al., 2020). A serious problem exists when even the most elite Black men must fight against racism in the workplace, which presents a barrier to their advancement. However, Black males from elite families still have advantages. Research has shown that successful Black elites had advantages such as previously having attended:

"elite private schools, membership in exclusive social organizations, and other types of connections that facilitate their knowledge of and entry into these jobs. The social networks formed in these settings help build the social and cultural capital that eases Black workers' entry into or maintenance of their elite standing" (Wingfield, 2014, p. 242).

However, the research did find that 75 percent of Black men reported having professional networks that are strong both within and outside of the workplace, but even strong networks have limitations due to systemic racism in the workplace (Spriggs et al., 2020). Research has shown that approximately 58 percent of men have been faced with racial prejudice in the workplace, as well as overt racial discrimination and hate crimes in the larger society. The worst forms of racial prejudice in the workplace include subtle microaggressions. Some of the microaggressions experienced by Black men in the workplace include deliberate discrimination based on actions or words, micro-insults that demean the men, lack of sensitivity, lack of validation, and even physical intimidation and violence. As a result, many Black men are seeking their own path via entrepreneurship in self-owned businesses (Spriggs et al., 2020).

Research has indicated that Black men are more likely to work in jobs that have higher stress, such as jobs involving shift work with high demands, longer hours, and limited control, increasing their risk for health problems

(Archibald, 2019). Black men are caught in a vicious cycle of performing the worst jobs in society. Black men are not only discriminated against in the workplace, but they also face discrimination in hiring practices or, due to their inability to enter higher educational institutions, are limited in their ability to acquire jobs that are not physically demanding and mentally stressful. For example, only 0.8 percent of Fortune 500 CEOs are Black men, only three percent are professionals, and only ten percent hold a college degree (Center for Talent and Innovation, 2019). Few Black men have access to senior leadership in their organization, making professional advancement challenging. In all areas of the United States, Black men are likely to experience racism between 44 and 79 percent. Examples of microaggressions experienced by Black men in the workplace include being told they are not articulate, having others take credit for their ideas, and being mischaracterized, overlooked, and ignored when there are opportunities to grow. Black men experience racially insensitive language (Center for Talent and Innovation, 2019).

Workplaces are not culturally sensitive to Black men. Black men cope with severe issues in today's world and workplace, and according to McCluney et al. (2017), Black individuals may often feel like calling in sick because of some act of violence against Black people in their community or city that creates a high level of fear. However, they are under "pressure to maintain a professional demeanor and carry out their regular work routines" (McCluney et al., 2017, p. 767). In other words, the experiences of Black men outside of their workplace may affect their workplace functioning, indicating the need for a psychologically safe work environment. When Black men call in to take a mental health day, it is often viewed as reflecting a low level of commitment, whereas a White person could call in, and it would be accepted, but when a Black man does the same, it is racialized. However, the reality is that when a Black man witnesses violence against Blacks in their city or community, they experience trauma that reflects a systemic issue affecting those men not only in society but also in the workplace (McCluney et al., 2017).

Consider the incident where Philando Castile was shot seven times by the police, which his fiancé in Minneapolis, Minnesota, filmed (McCluney et al., 2017). The video was streamed on Facebook with 3.2 million views in just the first 24 hours. This type of situation, when witnessed, results in a high level of racial trauma, making Black men feel unsafe due to the identity they share with the victims as Black men. Organizations have a unique opportunity to generate resources to counteract the adverse effects of traumatic events. However, creating social, material, and cognitive resources and building quality relationships within the organization are required. Organizations must ensure that their socialization practices view employees with compassion and that diverse views are integrated into strategic planning and thinking to address the trauma that Black employees face (McCluney et al., 2017).

However, organizations should go further and integrate diverse views into all strategic planning, which means that Black men should be engaged at all levels of the organization to ensure it is culturally responsive to their life and workplace situations (McCluney et al., 2017). It is necessary to create identity safety to ensure Black men can effectively function in the workplace in the absence of fear that their gender and race will make their experience threatening. Identity-safe organizations ensure that Black men can be productive and realize positive outcomes in their work. Furthermore, "psychologically safe environments increase an individual's sense of belonging, assuring people feel welcomed, supported, and valued" (McCluney et al., 2017, p. 776). When Black men do not feel psychologically safe in their workplace, they cannot develop the level of trust required to form social networks with their fellow employees.

Mentoring Supports Black Men to Advance in Professional Careers

Research shows that developing a professional identity is vital and is supported by mentoring (Hawkins, 2022; Palmer, 2008; Strayhorn & Johnson, 2020). Research was conducted to understand how Black men with doctoral degrees define their professional identity and the factors that helped them develop it (Strayhorn & Johnson, 2020). Not many Black men have achieved a doctoral degree, and research shows that only 35 percent of Black men who attend college reach that level in their profession. However, even Black men who have attained a doctoral degree may not perform well in their profession. Black men must develop a professional identity that supports them in achieving success. First, the individual must commit to behave morally and ethically and to feel high pride in their profession. When doctoral students acquire their degrees and develop a high level of socialization with those in their career field, it supports success. As Black men earn their doctoral degrees, they embrace their professional identity, which leads to stability, confidence, and clarity and allows them to internalize their professional identity (Strayhorn & Johnson, 2020). However, research has highlighted mentors' roles in developing a professional identity. As Black men interact meaningfully with other professionals in their career fields, their professional identity matures. However, with the high levels of discrimination Black men face in the workplace, identifying mentors may be problematic (Strayhorn & Johnson, 2020). The question then is where Black men can turn for the professional mentoring they so desperately need to succeed.

One study interviewing African American men and women revealed that all participants highlighted the significance of mentoring in their ability to develop within their careers and realize advancement (Palmer et al., 2008). For example, one participant, a Black male in his forties who has worked for the same company for two decades, stated the following concerning the significant importance of mentoring:

"Mentoring is absolutely essential because the mentor is the person who understands the culture, the business, and the climate of the organization. They understand what is required of a position. They are the ones who have the power to place people, to pull people up. Earlier in my career, I was very focused, very interested in looking for ways in which to discover the wealth of opportunities in the organization and how I could capitalize on those possibilities. And even with my high performance, it was not happening. So I believe my career would have been tremendously enhanced and would be further along if I had consistent mentoring throughout" (Palmer et al., 2008, p. 46).

Another Black male participant in the study expressed much the same and stated,

"I think if I had a person that we now have in charge of this division, who would have taken me under their wings and provided some mentoring, I would definitely be in senior management at this stage of my career, probably at the vice-president level. But when I encountered some people that could have mentored me, they were usually standoffish" (Palmer et al., 2008, p. 47).

The study concluded that the lack of formal mentoring hindered career advancement since all participants expressed that they would be further advanced in their careers with the guidance offered through mentoring (Palmer et al., 2008).

The reality is that organizations have overlooked mentoring and sponsorship's role in advancing Black men in the workplace (Hawkins, 2022). Organizational mentors and sponsors depend on personal connections and social networks to promote those they mentor to leadership positions; that approach has been shown in the research to exclude Black men. A study examined the daily challenges Black men experienced and their experiences with sponsorship and mentorship in their organization. The study involved nine Black male participants who were interviewed and belonged to the African American Chamber of Commerce and African American Strategy Group (AASC). All participants had earned a doctorate or master's degree and were between 41 and 60 (Hawkins, 2022). The study revealed that Black mentors provided positive mentoring relationships. Participant two in the study stated that his mentor's first advice to him:

"was that every time you were rejected, counseled or otherwise treated where you feel that you are not being treated fairly because the person may be a White male or White female and you are Black doesn't mean it's discrimination, but there are times when you have to speak up for not only yourself, sometimes for others, however, do not let it make you overly distracted, you owe it to yourself to keep performing and proving that you have what it takes and you deserve to be where you are, you are ready for that next level" (Hawkins, 2022, p. 105).

Another participant noted that their mentors advised them to "stand on your own, you know, on your own feet because not everyone is going to be an advocate for you in this agency" (Hawkins, 2022, p. 106). One participant revealed that "everyone came in with their own rose-colored goggles, that is everyone views life through their own experience, and so he gave me some excellent advice regarding race relations, and when to act and when not to act" (Hawkins, 2022, p. 107). The participants noted they could bounce ideas off their mentors, receive professional counseling, have discussions, make beneficial connections, and that mentors would point them in the right direction (Hawkins, 2022). The findings in the study highlight the importance of Black men having Black mentors, but since there are not always Black mentors in the workplace setting, a professional social network is needed to assist Black men to advance in their careers and cope with the workplace-related problems they experience.

Social Networking for Workplace Success

As noted, the African American Chamber of Commerce and African American Strategy Group (AASC) provides a social network for Black men. It is in Cincinnati, Ohio, and offers business training to various organizations, including counseling and training services (AASC, 2024). Another option for networking for Black men is the 100 Black Men of America, Inc. organization, with 100 chapters that mentor young Black males to prepare them for success during and after school. However, these types of programs are not available in every city and community in the United States, so Black men are left to develop their own social networks to assist them in workplace and professional development. A recent study sought to build a social network at multiple levels as an intervention to promote Black men's health (Harley et al., 2020). Although the focus of this chapter is not on the health of Black men, the study provides valuable insights into how a social network can be constructed for Black men (Harley et al., 2020).

The construction of the social network relied on a partnership between organizations in the community and the academic university setting (Harley et al., 2020). The intervention involved a monthly meeting for Black men to facilitate discussions about their experiences and highlighted the "tremendous isolation and the need for safe spaces for men to connect and express their authentic selves" (Harley et al., 2020, p. 3). The recommendations that arose from the discussion emphasized the need for community and social connections to support mentoring and assist in exploring leadership opportunities (Harley et al., 2020). The same type of groups can be formed to assist

Black men with workplace difficulties, and they need mentors to guide them in navigating those difficulties. These groups can be formed at the community or city level and help Black men connect with older, more experienced Black men who can offer mentoring. Beginning with peer support groups and inviting older, successful Black men into the discussions can help Black men connect with one another and with mentors who can help them not only navigate challenging workplaces characterized by systemic racism but also help them advance in their careers. Unfortunately, there is a shortage of research on how Black men develop social networks in the workplace; however, Wingfield (2014) conducted a study involving 42 Black males employed in various professional fields.

The participants revealed that during their work history, they had been employed in environments where they were the only Black male or were among only two or three Black men, with all their colleagues being White men (Wingfield, 2014). However, the Black men revealed that their social networks included White men who had mentored them. One participant revealed that "developing interracial social networks with White peers is critical to professional success" (Wingfield, 2014, p.

246). Another participant stated that a White man was his mentor and "He actually helped recruit me here and said, I want to help you grow and develop this department. He looks out for me and does the things you want a mentor to do – sort of look for opportunity, feedback, I'd do this differently and this kind of thing, and be honest and open about it" (Wingfield, 2014, p. 246).

Developing social networks for Black men was a gendered process. It enabled the participants to interact easily by forming social ties through shared hobbies and pastimes and using masculinized behaviors that helped them overcome the racial barriers within the workplace. Therefore, "gender solidarity facilitated the development of these men's interracial social networks" (Wingfield, 2014, p. 246). The Black male participants broke down the racial barriers by discussing sports or other masculine interests. Working out with White coworkers also helped cross racial barriers for Black men and assisted them in building social networks (Wingfield, 2014). This study indicated that Black men should work to develop social networks across racial boundaries to assist them in career development and advancement.

However, it would be remiss not to include an examination of Black churches' role in creating social networks for Black men. Church-based social networks are essential resources for African Americans and Black men (Nguyen et al., 2016). The family solidarity model assess family cohesion and relations and is essential in conceptualizing the aspects of family social ties. However, this also includes extended family and may consist of those in the community who are seen as family, such as fellow church members. Previous research has explored various social networks but has done so by examining them individually rather than how they tie together and form "constellations of social network characteristics in a more holistic manner" (Nguyen et al., 2016, p. 703). The failure to examine the multiple aspects of social networks among Black males overlooks the role that churches and other community organizations play. Barber (2014) analyzed the role that the contemporary Black church plays in the public realm, specifically in its provision of opportunities and resources, and found that as the Black church interacts with organizations, it helps to support Black men and boys in succeeding in various areas of their lives.

Black churches are positioned to address problems with unemployment among Black men, as well as other areas that assist them in acquiring gainful employment. Specifically, mentorship within the Black church helps Black men to develop their capacities and provides spiritual and emotional support for them to navigate the difficulties of the workplace.

However, as Barber (2014) noted, Black churches cannot solve all Black men's problems, but by becoming actively involved in the public realm, they have the power to make a difference. The Black church is central to the lives of the majority of Black males, and it has historically and traditionally offered support in the areas of informational and emotional support, as well as provided advice and counseling (Nguyen et al., 2020). Building support networks for Black men to assist them in advancing in the workplace and coping with the discrimination they face makes the Black church a critical aspect in the lives of those men. Research shows that Black men and African Americans generally rely on the church's support networks (Nguyen et al., 2020). The prominence of the church among Black men means it is ideally situated to drive initiatives within the community to support Black men and boys by partnering with other organizations to ensure that they have the support they need to advance in the workplace and to support them in overcoming challenging work conditions characterized by systemic racism and discrimination.

Summary

The information presented in this chapter reveals how Black men struggle in the workplace to succeed and advance in an environment of systemic racism and discrimination, which is still, to some extent, racially segregated. Black men have difficulties in advancing to managerial and professional roles and generally hold high-stress, risky jobs requiring shift work, which are lower-paid and lower-status positions than those of White men. Even Black men from the most elite and wealthy families face these same problems despite the advantages of attending the best colleges and universities. The types of discrimination in the workplace include blatant discrimination and more low-key types of discrimination, such as microaggressions.

Although some progress has been made as more Black men are attending college, once they graduate, they face discrimination in hiring practices. Once hired, they enter a workplace that is not culturally sensitive to Black men and their struggles. Mentors assist Black men in developing their professional identity. As the information in this chapter reveals, in the absence of mentoring, Black men do not progress as far in their careers as they otherwise could have if they had mentors.

Social networking is vital for Black men and may involve connections with organizations that advance them. However, Black men must take the initiative to form social networks within the workplace, which means crossing cultural and racial boundaries. This could involve establishing connections with colleagues of other races in a way that bridges cultural gaps.

The Black church is vital for social networking. It has the power to play a critical role in developing opportunities for social networking by working and partnering with organizations in the community to help Black men connect with others in the community, as well as supporting programs that help those men connect with others who can serve as mentors. As the Black church partners with organizations and universities, it will be possible to build awareness of the importance of mentoring for Black men to help them advance in their careers, and it will further inform organizations of the necessary cultural sensitivity required in the workplace to open doors to the advancement of Black men.

The following chapter will examine the physical health disparities affecting Black men and the importance of healthcare access and preventive measures.

Chapter Nine

Health and Wellness

This book has examined various aspects of the lives of Black men that must be integrated into their potential for healing. The information in this chapter will examine the physical health disparities affecting Black men and the importance of access and preventive measures. Black men are often viewed by the healthcare system and others they encounter within the system "as a stereotype or caricature" (Gilbert et al., 2019, p. 2). Research on the health of Black men has had a relatively narrow focus, making it essential that there be a more broad and in-depth examination of their health outcomes to assist in comprehending how institutional forces and social experiences affect those outcomes (Gilbert et al., 2019; Jack & Griffith, 2016).

Physical Health Disparities Affecting Black Men

African Americans have generally suffered worse health outcomes historically, and the same is true for Black males, who generally have shorter lifespans than White males or even Black females (Gilbert et al., 2019). Black men have the worst overall health of any other groups within the United States and die more than seven years earlier than all races of women as well as die younger than all races of men (Gilbert et al., 2019). Currently, White men have an average life span of 67.6 years, whereas, for Black men, it is 60.7 years, so the lifespan of Black men is lower than that of White men (Gilbert et al., 2019; Jack & Griffith, 2016). Black women live on average 4.7 years longer than Black men (Gilbert et al., 2019).

The leading causes of death among Black men include heart disease, at a rate of 24.8 percent; cancer, at a rate of 23 percent; unintentional injuries, at a rate of 5.8 percent; and homicide, at a rate of 4.3 percent (Pathak, 2017). However, Black men also experience high rates of diabetes and heart disease (Jack & Griffith, 2019; Pathak, 2017).

AIDS is also higher among Black men than men of other races (Gilbert et al., 2019).

Premature deaths among young Black males are linked to the absence of fathers in the home (Jones-Eversley et al., 2020). Additionally, young Black males are at an increased risk of dying due to homicide, reported at approximately 81 per 100,000 deaths among Black men of that age (Jones-Eversley et al., 2020). Suicides among young Black males are also more common than among other groups and are stated at 93.5 deaths per 100,000 (Jones-Eversley et al., 2020). It is problematic that Black men are much more likely than other races of men to have poorly managed or undiagnosed chronic illnesses, such as heart disease, diabetes, and cancer, which shorten their life spans (Gilbert et al., 2019).

Delay in seeking treatment is mainly due to the fact that many Black men possess a lower socioeconomic status than White men, making Black men more likely to die from illness and chronic disease (Gilbert et al., 2019). Research shows that the income of Black men has not kept up with the income of White men, placing them at a unique disadvantage in receiving regular healthcare (Gilbert et al., 2019).

Black men are essentially invisible in their communities because so many are incarcerated or have died young (Gilbert et al., 2019). Black men are also uncounted in communities, so the needs of the community are not adequately reflected to address the needs of Black men, who generally do not participate in civic life or employment, especially following incarceration. Therefore, many Black men exist on the borders of the community, hidden and unaccounted for in terms of their needs.

However, "attention to the health of Black men tends to fall between research on racial and ethnic disparities and men's health. In research on health disparities, there is a need to look beyond race and ethnicity to consider gender and other factors that shape psychological and social experiences" (Gilbert et al., 2019, p. 5). The need to examine this way aligns with the focus of this book, which examines issues surrounding Black men from an intersectional view of how race and gender intersect to affect the experiences of Black men. Gilbert et al. (2019) noted that the "intersectional racialized and gendered approach to understanding the social, economic, and health trajectories of Black men offers a framework for understanding the systemic and structural barriers that limit them from optimizing their chances to live long, healthy lives" (p. 6).

Challenges and Barriers to Healthcare Access

The social narrative that is all too common is that Black men are violent and dangerous rather than being viewed as humans who experience a vast array of disparities (Jones Eversley et al., 2020). The same social narrative influences the information and formation of public policy and the practices used in law enforcement, emphasizing incarceration rather than considering therapy to support Black men (Jones-Eversley et al., 2020).

Those social narratives may serve as a barrier to Black men seeking healthcare provision due to their distrust of the system and their trepidations about how they will be treated within the healthcare system (Jones-Eversley et al., 2020). Medical mistrust is a phenomenon where Black men lack trust in general in the healthcare system, including institutions, providers, and any treatment plans (Jordan et al., 2024).

Medical mistrust arises typically and historically from the view of Black men and how the providers are not aligned with their culture, combined with potential provider bias (Jordan et al., 2024). Medical mistrust has a long-standing existence among Black men, who have typically experienced mistreatment and discrimination within systems and institutions (Jordan et al., 2024). When those structural and systemic barriers are not considered in policy and by healthcare organizations, it will be impossible to remove the barriers to Black men seeking healthcare. This is unfortunate, since the high rates of educational underachievement, combined with health behaviors such as smoking and health issues such as cardiovascular disease, may lead to premature death (Jones-Eversley et al., 2020).

Structural barriers include high unemployment rates among Black men, many living in poverty, and the lack of health insurance (Connell et al., 2019). In rural areas, medical specialties are lacking, and transportation problems are associated with accessing healthcare services (Connell et al., 2019). Research indicates that Black men do not seek healthcare because of the cultural norms existing in the African American community (Eley et al., 2019). For example,

"Beliefs about masculinity and manhood are rooted deep in culture... play a role in shaping the behavioral patterns of men in ways that have consequences for health. Men are socialized to project strength, individuality, autonomy, dominance, stoicism, and physical aggression, and to avoid demonstrations of emotion or vulnerability that could be construed as weakness" (Williams, 2003, p. 726).

The cultural norms result in Black men having fewer healthcare system encounters, resulting in delays in seeking treatment once they have developed symptoms, lack of compliance with medication, and an overall hesitance to discuss their health issues (Eley et al., 2019). Research has shown that Black men with Type 2 Diabetes fail to seek treatment because of their intense focus on what they perceive as masculine behavior. The masculine behavior results in Black men desiring to maintain control over their bodies regardless of the medical outcomes, and limits the level of social support they are willing to accept.

Eley et al. (2019) conducted 40 focus group studies with 310 Black men in North Carolina to examine their health-seeking behaviors. They discovered that female family members had the most influence on Black men's willingness to seek healthcare (Eley et al., 2019). If female family members encouraged Black men to seek healthcare, they were more likely to reach out for care (Eley et al., 2019). Alternatively, lack of support from female family members lowered the willingness of Black men to seek medical care. Children were also an excellent motivator for Black men seeking medical care, primarily when encouraged. However, children also worked as passive motivators. Parents also influence whether Black men are willing to seek medical care, and the study found that parents have a significant impact on the willingness of Black men to seek healthcare (Eley et al., 2019).

However, family and cultural norms also had an influence on Black men regarding seeking medical care (Eley et al., 2019). For example, if a Black man's father was hesitant to seek healthcare, it is more likely that he will follow his father's example and be less willing. The gender norms were also found to impact healthcare-seeking among Black men because they embraced the idea that they need to be strong and tough.

The study found that the peers of Black men influence their willingness to seek healthcare. Community influences are also crucial in determining Black men's willingness to seek medical care. As the community provides healthcare information, Black men become more acclimated to the need for medical care. The study noted that teachers and preachers in the community can positively influence Black men in seeking medical care, as well as anyone else whom the Black community holds in high regard. One participant stated:

"Just like last year, I was in nursing school, and we had to test each other's blood pressure. Mine came back 165 over 135. My teacher told me to get the hell out of her classroom. She said it just like that, 'Go to the doctor.' And I went, 'No, I'll be all right.' She was like, 'No.' And if I don't go, I wasn't welcome back in class. She told me to go to the hospital, 'cause she said I was on the verge of having a stroke. And ever since then, I'm on blood pressure meds" (Eley et al., 2019, p. 7).

It was noted that even news media and celebrities can positively impact Black men's views of seeking healthcare (Eley et al., 2019). One participant stated,

"The radio, Michael Baisden, he had influenced me to go check my prostate out, listening to him. On the media... I think I've seen one commercial with this African American male talking about prostate cancer and the effects, and he was saying, 'Had I checked it out earlier, I would've known. I may have lived a bit longer" (Eley et al., 2019, p. 7).

However, it was also noted that mass media campaigns and public service announcements can influence Black men's views on seeking the medical care they need (Eley et al., 2019). The study concluded that:

"social relationships are important influences on the health and healthcare-seeking behaviors of African American men and go further to delineate the nature of influences across relationship types, both in direct provision of information and support and in the indirect messages they send" (Eley et al., 2019, p. 7).

The findings presented by Eley et al. (2019) emphasize the influence that partners, parents, children, and peers have on Black men's willingness to seek medical care, but it also highlights the importance of mass media and public service information.

A separate study stated the same findings and noted how interpersonal barriers stand in the way of Black men seeking healthcare services (Connell et al., 2019). The study was conducted in Mississippi among Black men and revealed how interpersonal influences affect Black men's healthcare services-seeking behavior. Black men have distrust for healthcare service providers and insurance companies, making the prevention of disease a low priority based on the idea that they hold the responsibility to provide rather than being provided to.

Another factor that serves as a barrier is fear, noted to be prevalent among the participants in the study, specifically fear associated with receiving a bad diagnosis or learning that they are severely ill. Black men also fear stigmatization in their community because they believe they will be seen as weak or less than what they should be as men. Illness is viewed among many Black men as a personal failure. One participant stated, "I don't know if we're afraid of the stigma of being sick or don't want people to think we're weak" (Connell et al., 2019, p. 8).

The participants' medical distrust was highlighted in the statements of one participant: "They got these medical companies that are going to give kickbacks. So they don't care what prescription you take" (Connell et al., 2019, p. 8). However, the participants did reveal that when they encountered a provider who was empathetic and showed a personal interest in them, they were more willing to seek healthcare services.

Disease prevention was found as a low priority among the Black men in the study, based on the idea of their responsibility to take care of their family and cope with daily stress, such as paying the bills (Connell et al., 2019).

Black men may use alternative methods to cope with their health, such as spirituality and religion (Connell et al., 2019). Rather than using preventive healthcare services, they are more likely than 43% of other men to rely on the emergency room (ER) for healthcare rather than seeking doctor or clinic appointments (Connell et al., 2019). There is a need to overcome the cultural and gender barriers, and create a positive discussion around healthcare for Black men. There is a need to normalize seeking healthcare for Black men. In a society that has traditionally and historically placed them on the border of society, this needs to change, to ensure that Black men feel welcome in the healthcare environment and that barriers are removed.

Importance of Prevention

Black men have been found to refuse to seek medical care until a critical incident occurs (Connell et al., 2019). However, among Black men, those with higher levels of education are more likely to seek preventive healthcare. Black men who are religiously affiliated also tend to seek preventive healthcare services at higher rates (Jordan et al., 2024). However, married Black men were shown in one study to be less likely to seek preventive healthcare services, but those with higher incomes were more likely to seek preventive healthcare services (Jordan et al., 2024). Decreased engagement of Black men in preventive healthcare services is linked to medical mistrust (Jordan et al., 2024). However, prevention is critically vital among Black men due to the health risks they face.

The University of Alabama, and the Center for Healthy African American Men through Partnerships

(CHAAMPS), and researchers at the University of Minnesota worked together to explore the health disparities among Black men (Shikany et al., 2018). The focus of the study was identifying the behavioral, socioeconomic, and biological factors that continue to drive Black men's health disparities (Shikany et al., 2018).

The researchers revealed that the importance of preventive healthcare for Black men is due to a more considerable chronic disease burden, such as Type 2 Diabetes, (which is two times higher than among White men) (Shikany et al., 2018). Cardiovascular disease is also higher among Black men, and they are 80% more likely to have a stroke than White men. Black men also have higher rates of cancer than White men, especially prostate cancer (Okoro et al., 2020; Shikany et al., 2018). The World Health Organization has highlighted health disparities and how the social determinants of health impact the population (Shikany et al., 2018).

The social determinants of health are "the circumstances in which people are born, grow up, live, work, and age" (Shikany et al., 2018, p. 2). As already reviewed in this book, Black men are more likely to reside in areas that are unhealthy — particularly in rural areas where chemical pollution is not highly regulated, making their chance of developing diseases, including cancer, more likely. Black men living in poverty are at an increased risk of disease because they do not have access to healthy housing, food, and water. When all the social determinants of health for Black men are combined, it creates a dangerous brew for the potential for serious health conditions, making preventive healthcare critical. However, the question is: how Black men can be encouraged and motivated toward preventive healthcare?

Interventions to Support Black Men in Seeking Healthcare and Preventive Services

Okoro et al. (2020) sought to determine how a community-engaged intervention could support Black men seeking preventive healthcare. The intervention involved a partnership with the local National Association for the Advancement of Colored People (NAACP). Fliers were used to recruit Black males for the meetings. The community sessions involved presenting Black men with information on diabetes, prostate cancer, and other health issues, such as cardiovascular disease, and healthy meals were served to model the best healthy foods for the participants. Local healthcare providers were also involved in the intervention. The program impacted Black men by providing them with increased awareness of health risks and increased knowledge. The program was found to change Black men's attitudes about seeking healthcare. The program supported increased Black men's self-efficacy around engagement in the healthcare system and supported lifestyle changes while building a sense of social support and community (Okoro et al., 2020).

The attitude changes are significant in this type of intervention because of the propensity of African American men to be unlikely to seek medical care regularly unless a condition becomes critical (Okoro et al., 2020). The intervention increased the resolve of the Black men who participated in seeking care more proactively and regularly. Increasing the level of self-efficacy that Black men possessed assisted the participants in obtaining more information about how to navigate the healthcare system and feeling more empowered to become actively involved in their healthcare by setting appointments and asking the providers questions during their visits.

However, one of the most critical aspects of the intervention was building community support among Black men — enabling them to connect and nurture one another in their support group to transform their thinking about preventive healthcare actions. One participant stated,

"We were really trying to communicate not only in terms of learnin' for ourselves, but create an opportunity to interact with each other. This community is disconnected, it's a transit community, and so many people don't know each other. I think it's been able to create a support system that we can fellowship and encourage each other" (Okoro et al., 2020, p. 7).

The participants reported that the community support group made them understand that they were not alone, and helped them gain feedback from other Black men (Okoro et al., 2020). The interactive learning environment in the groups was assisted by visual aids that stimulated discussion among the participants. One participant revealed that Black men,

"Keep most things inside, to ourselves. It's helpful to get outside of yourself and discuss it with other men who are in your same situation, or you might be in their situation. A lot of information came from the older men that were in their 60s and 70s having experienced those things personally, which leads you to see that you might not want to experience those, and if you do, you see that there's light at the end of the tunnel for those... if you do have a problem" (Okoro et al., 2020, p. 8).

This study, along with other information reviewed, highlights the critical need for the involvement of family, partners, children, friends, and the community in encouraging and supporting Black men to seek healthcare services for prevention, regular checkups, and care for their conditions. However, some measures should be taken among healthcare providers to engage Black men. A cultural change is required in the healthcare system to acknowledge the diversity of patients and providers. (Beverley et al., 2022). The acknowledgment of the diversity of patients must be accompanied by training for healthcare service providers. Firstly, training must be provided for cultural sensitivity and patient engagement so providers will understand the specific needs and communication methods of Black men, who often fail to come out and say what they really mean or do not express their lack of understanding about what the provider is saying (Beverley et al., 2022).

Oftentimes, health providers make assumptions about Black men, believing they are not smart enough to grasp what is being said about their health issues or assuming that because their literacy is low, their intellectual capacity is also low (Beverley et al., 2022). Healthcare providers must receive training so that Black men are not labeled, for example, as non-compliant, without asking them why they did not follow directions or medication instructions, as this inquiry can provide simple solutions. Healthcare providers must also receive training to understand how spirituality and religion affect the beliefs of Black men about healthcare services. A SPOT framework is recommended, which involves (1) Speaking to patients to understand their specific situation, (2) Pacifying any factors related to fear, (3) Outlining what the individuals hold as important, and (4) Taking into consideration the time needed by the patient to accept their diagnosis of a disease (Beverley et al., 2022). Ensuring healthcare access and preventive treatment for Black men requires interventions, support, and changes in how healthcare providers engage them.

Summary

Black men fail to seek healthcare services due to mistrust and their idea of masculinity. However, the people in Black men's lives significantly influence their healthcare-seeking behaviors. All the social determinants of health must be addressed for Black men, which means engagement and partnerships among all healthcare service providers and organizations in the community are required. A community initiative opens the door to creating positive discussions around healthcare services, helping to overcome the masculinity and stoicism that Black men try to maintain in their lives. Furthermore, community interventions can help Black men overcome their mistrust of the healthcare system and providers because, as those providers present information in interventions, familiarity develops, and rapport can be constructed. Bringing the healthcare of Black men to the forefront of the healthcare discussion and provision requires the involvement of actors at every level within the community and the healthcare system to ensure they feel free to admit they have health issues. When they do, providers must be engaged and interested in helping them. Healthcare providers need education and training to ensure they provide culturally appropriate care and view Black men as human beings rather than relying on typical stereotypes and caricatures that have for too long permeated American society.

Chapter Ten

Spirituality, Religion, Faith, and the Resilience of Black Men

This book has examined various factors that present unique challenges in the lives of Black men, how those challenges can be overcome, and how barriers can be addressed. However, it would be remiss to fail to examine the role that spirituality, religion, and faith play in developing resilience among Black men. Therefore, this chapter will explore the role of spirituality and religious practices in the lives of Black men and how faith communities provide support and foster resilience. It is common knowledge that the Black church has historically and traditionally been central to the lives of the Black population. During the days of slavery, the Black church provided respite from daily abuse and discrimination and serves as a place where Black people could gather to worship God and offer many forms of support to one another. Since this chapter examines how spirituality and faith build resilience among Black men, it is necessary to define spirituality and religion.

Spirituality is defined “as a belief in a sacred, transcendent force that permeates all beings and influences all aspects of lived experiences” (Mattis & Grayman-Simpson, 2013, p. 547). Spirituality has also been defined “as an internal process of seeking personal authenticity, genuineness, and wholeness as an aspect of identity development” (Allen, 2022, p. 1). In other words, spirituality speaks to the development of inner strength. Religion has been defined by African American adults “as one’s adherence to the prescribed beliefs and devotional practices associated with the worship of God” (Mattis & Grayman-Simpson, 2013, p. 547). Therefore, religion speaks to the affiliation with a set of beliefs. Religion and spirituality are linked to African Americans’ physical, mental, relational, community, and political health (Mattis & Grayman-Simpson, 2013). Although spirituality and religion are distinct, the two are inherently linked in Black culture.

The Psychology of Spirituality, Religion, and Resilience

The field of psychology has explored how spirituality and religion build resilience among individuals. One study examined the relationship between religion, spirituality, and resilience (Schwalm et al., 2021). After reviewing 44 studies in a systematic review, a moderate correlation was found between religion, spirituality and resilience, particularly among the high-quality studies. The subgroup analyses showed that spirituality was more strongly correlated than religion to resilience. The study noted that research with more than 1,500 participants combined showed the same findings. Further, it was revealed that the mechanisms for the relationship are not known but can be explained partially "by the existence of common factors underlying resilience and religious/spiritual qualities, such as optimism, positive emotions, social support, and the search for meaning and purpose" (Schwalm et al., 2021, p. 8).

Positive religious coping has been shown in research to be linked to a better psychological adjustment that assists in problem-solving and coping with stress (Park et al., 2017). Positive religious coping has likewise been linked to better levels of well-being. However, it is unfortunate that research on religious coping among African Americans in general, and specifically among males, has been largely overlooked in research, which is noted as surprising due to the integral role that spirituality and religion play in the lives of African Americans (Park et al., 2017).

Importance of Religion and Spirituality in the Lives of Black Men

Religion and spirituality have an enormous influence on the culture of Black individuals, with approximately 70 percent claiming they are religious and spiritual (English, 2016). The religious expression of Black people is rooted in a society that was historically hostile in the United States, specific to slavery and segregation. As such, religious expression assisted African Americans in addressing the issues that harmed their well-being

(English, 2016). Black spirituality has its roots in African spirituality and American slavery and provided slaves with "a musical symphony of hope through the creation of Negro spirituals, and became the catalyst for spiritual leaders, which flourished in an environment of struggle and conflict from the 16th through the 20th century" (Allen, 2022, pp. 1-2). Black religious institutions offer robust support systems and are essential resources in the Black community (English, 2016).

Churches in the Black community provide various forms of assistance, including food, transportation, money, fellowship, spiritual and emotional support, and a sense of belonging (English, 2016). The Black church plays a vital role in the community during times of hardship, including illness and death (English, 2016). Spirituality and religion impact Black individuals' adjustment through various phases of their lives, from college education to the professional work setting (English, 2016).

Research has shown that spirituality and religion positively influence better academic performance among Black students (English, 2016). Additionally, spirituality gives Black men a sense of purpose and supports their resilience (English, 2016). Spirituality supports Black men in developing leadership strengths since those who demonstrate substantial spiritual growth also develop higher levels in leadership development (Allen, 2022). The Black church is the cornerstone of African American communities and has guided Black males in navigating the world (Salinas et al.,2018). Black men have been acknowledged in research to rely on their religious and spiritual beliefs in the face of challenges and adversity and to make their daily decisions (Salinas et al., 2018). Research has also shown that Black men generally believe that God is in control of their destinies (Salinas et al., 2018).

A separate study that examined the sources of stress for Black men and the tools they use to cope with stressors undertook a community-partnered participatory research approach with 295 Black men (Chung et al., 2014). The study found that more than 93 percent of the participants reported dealing with stress related to economic challenges and racism. Other forms of stress include relationships, children, and health or illness. However, racism-associated stress was reported at a higher rate than other forms of stress among the participants, including disrespect, denial of their rights, and the prevalence of criminality and violence in the Black community. Of the participants who stated racism as a severe source of stress, more than 68 percent identified institutional racism, with lower percentages reporting personal or internalized racism, at 31 percent and 13 percent, respectively. When asked how they coped with stressors, God or the church was cited by 42.1 percent of the participants, and family and friends were cited by 27.6 percent of the participants, highlighting the crucial nature of the religious family and community in ensuring the resilience of Black men (Chung et al., 2014).

The focus of African American families on spirituality has been passed through many generations to assist them in coping and to provide hope. The Black church increases the family's reach to the larger community (Salinas et al., 2018). A study was conducted among twelve Black male students in a college setting in Florida who were between 19 and 39 years of age. Focus groups were conducted to understand the role of spirituality and religion in the students' lives. The key theme that was identified in the participants' responses was that the Black male participants described the Bible as the model they followed for masculinity and manhood. One participant noted, "What I learned of becoming a man is basically the Word of God" (Salinas et al., 2018, p. 9). Another participant revealed, "The word of God changed me as well, and I became more humble. The word of God taught me how to become a right man" (Salinas et al., 2018, p. 9). The participants also identified Jesus as their role model for leadership and the church as a vital source of leadership development that assists them in functioning in their divine purpose (Salinas et al., 2018).

The integral nature of the church in developing resilience among Black men cannot be understated. One study interviewing 30 Black men found that spirituality and religion assisted them in overcoming obstacles (Salinas et al., 2018). The participants expressed how they relied on spirituality and religion to give them the strength they needed to overcome adversities. Spirituality and religion relieved them of stress, offered comfort, and provided guidance and emotional support that assisted them in coping with challenges (Salinas et al., 2018). One participant revealed that spirituality fueled his ability to overcome challenges; another stated that prayer was essential for overcoming life challenges. One participant indicated that he knew God loved him even if others did not (Salinas et al., 2018).

A separate study identified suicidal thoughts as prevalent among Black men and sought to understand how they cope with those thoughts and develop resilience to overcome that mindset (Reed & Adams, 2020). Suicide is not discussed broadly in Black communities because it is seen as taboo, and a belief is held that African Americans just do not commit suicide. The study involved interviews with social workers, and one revealed the following experience:

"In 2017, while working for an outpatient mental health clinic in the Greater Washington Region, I became acquainted with a family of seven on the brink of homelessness. The oldest, a 17-year-old African American male, felt like he had the world on his shoulders. His family would eventually get split between several relatives' homes. In one sense, this provided a sense of stability and security, but at the same time, it produced anxiety because his concern was for his younger siblings. One evening, this young male attempted to take his life by cutting himself. He was admitted into a psychiatric hospital for one week and stabilized. Upon his discharge, we processed everything that occurred. He admitted that he wanted to die but reflected upon what he learned in the Black church. As a devout Baptist, he remembered the proselytization that taught he cannot enter the Kingdom of Heaven if he took his own life. Taking that teaching to heart, he used it as an opportunity to build on the resiliency that spirituality afforded this young man. He was able to identify the strengths within himself and use them when he experiences mood swings" (Reed & Adams, 2020, pp. 4-5).

The interviews with the social workers in the study revealed the powerful role that the church and spirituality play in the lives of Black men due to the social cohesiveness within the Black church and the spiritual guidance they receive (Reed & Adams, 2020).

The Black Church and Resilience

The Black church plays multiple roles in the lives of Black men and serves "as a primary agent of socialization" (Salinas et al., 2018, p. 3). The Black church not only provides support in various areas within Black communities but is viewed by African Americans as an extension of their family (Salinas et al., 2018). The Black church supports spiritual family values, creates a sense of spirituality that grounds African Americans, and helps them resist the oppression and dehumanization often present in society (Salinas et al., 2018).

Historically, Black churches were the only communal institutions in Black communities, both rural and urban, and they worked as an extended family (Lincoln & Mamiya, 1990). The relationships between churches and Black families are interactive and dynamic (Lincoln & Mamiya, 1990). In the early years, families served as the Black church's building blocks, and the church was the glue between families and the community (Lincoln & Mamiya, 1990). Historically and in the present, Black churches provide spiritual uplift and vital social occasions for meeting and interaction (Lincoln & Mamiya, 1990). Some Black churches sponsor recreational events, as well as athletic teams, and provide venues for various public functions (Lincoln & Mamiya, 1990). However, besides spreading the gospel of Jesus Christ, churches offer role models for Black children and youth (Lincoln & Mamiya, 1990). The involvement in church during childhood, and the support provided by the church indicate the reason that spirituality and religion are viewed by Black men as critical coping mechanisms that assist them in being resilient.

Despite the role that spirituality and religion play in the resilience of Black men, evidenced in the studies reviewed, research shows that church attendance has fallen among Black men (Tate, 2023). However, Tate (2023) sought to examine that phenomenon and conducted a study among 65 Black millennials to explore the church's role in their lives today compared to the historical Black church and its provision of socio-cultural resources. The participants revealed that attending church had both community development and social network benefits. For example, one participant stated,

> "In my city, which is a city that's mostly white, more than probably 80% white, there are fewer Black churches. And I kind of really wanted to be in a Black church because I was around White people all day. I was the only Black person at work" (Tate, 2023, p. 8).

Another participant also cited the importance of the Black church in their lives and described it as a place of refuge (Tate, 2023). Participants revealed that attending the Black church assisted Black Christians in supporting the positive development of their racial identity. One participant noted,

"Making friends at church – sometimes friends that turn to family. And just having a support system, kind of like a group of like-minded people. Like, you can go hang out with these people, and it's not going to get crazy or anything like that" (Tate, 2023, p. 9).

The participants also noted that the Black church provides them with older mentors who can help them navigate their faith and life (Tate, 2023). One participant stated, "For me, that makes the church community experience an irreplaceable one" (Tate, 2023, p. 9). The Black church enables members to share cultural resources, including opportunities, and supports its members in developing friendships based on faith. Although some research indicates that Black millennials are critical of the church, the reality is that it does not lead to disengagement because they place a high value on affiliation with the Black church and view it as an irreplaceable factor in their lives. The difference between older members in the Black church and Black millennials is that the older members see the church as a way to help them survive, while millennials see the Black church as a way to flourish (Tate, 2023). One participant revealed how he felt about church and its impact on his life as follows:

"When I think of my religion, my Christianity, it's really about how to be the best version of myself. And so, I see the church almost like a workshop where I can go and workshop myself. And so, I can go to church and think about the different ways I can negotiate difficult relationships, how I can negotiate my personal life, my work life. How I can negotiate my feelings of anxiety. Like it doesn't replace therapy, and I think the pastor at my church now would even say you still need to go to therapy, but hearing other people relate and tell you stories about how they've dealt with stuff and how they're still dealing with stuff and the strategies they use is never not helpful" (Tate, 2023, p. 15).

The statement of the Black male participant reveals how spirituality and religion assist Black men in various areas of their lives, navigating difficulties and building resilience, specifically among a community of like-minded people. The experience of worshipping with others, particularly the socio-emotional function, has psychological benefits. For example, one participant revealed how interactions with other church members helped him to receive spiritual replenishment each week (Tate, 2023). Black men who attend Black churches develop religious resilience, described as the ability to cope with changes in their political, racial, and social landscape. Religious resilience provides a framework to understand the Black church's dynamic role in Black men's lives (Tate, 2023).

However, despite the benefits of the Black church in developing resilience among Black men, research does show a decrease in church attendance among younger Black men, indicating the need for the Black church to create a more engaging environment where younger Black men can feel a sense of belonging (Combest, 2022). Engaging younger Black men in the Black church has the potential to support them in developing mental, social, and economic resilience as they are supported by older members who can serve as mentors (Combest, 2022). In my Doctor of Ministry dissertation, I explored spiritual formation and soul care in the Black church and developed a program that could guide Black churches in that endeavor. In today's world, characterized by racism, discrimination, and violence toward Black men, the Black church has the potential to serve as a critical source to help Black men develop higher levels of spiritual resilience in responding to their challenges in life.

Younger Black men whose family attends church are more likely to be involved; however, the Black church must provide more opportunities for engagement for young Black men (Combest, 2022). In a study that interviewed six Black men to understand what draws them to church, spirituality, family, and relationships with others in the church were cited as crucial. Relationships were the number one reason young Black men attended church. One participant stated, "The church, to me, is a support system to help me find my way when I am upset or troubled" (Combest, 2022, p. 61). Another participant revealed that church "establishes a foundation of what to believe. It also helps bring you joy by connecting with others and allows you to build on that when you leave" (Combest, 2022, p. 61). Yet another participant noted that the Black church provides "a place where you can connect with God. There is always a sense of energy among the people" (Combest, 2022, p. 61). The participants revealed that encouragement from their family and friends would make them more likely to attend church when disengaged. Every participant in the study, except for one, stated that they greatly desired to participate in the Black church and engage more fully. The participants described the church community as integral in their lives, comparing it to a village or a family (Combest, 2022).

Also covered in my doctoral dissertation is the need for community bonds among Black church members and the surrounding community, requiring relationship building. One study reported using the Black Love, Activism, and Community (BLAC) model to build resilience and healing in the Black community (Turner et al., 2022). The BLAC model identified four domains of resilience that are grounded in the Black culture, including (1) relationships, (2) spirituality, (3) identity, and (4) active expression, cited as crucial aspects of healing and serving as protective factors. Relationships within Black communities set a foundation for spiritual and emotional love based on faith. It is noted that "the psychology of resistance to oppression suggests that participation in activism is a path to positive psychological outcomes such as self-esteem" (Turner et al., 2022, p. 549). Community bonds positively impact flourishing, self-actualization, and hope. Although this chapter does not center on activism, it is notable that as loving and caring community relationships develop based on the love of God, it enables the Black community in general and Black men specifically to build networks of support aligning with the African American collectivist-communal orientation within the cultural traditions of that population, both traditionally and historically. The principles that emerge from Black spirituality and traditions of wisdom support a pathway to well-being for Black men and may include principles of balance, creativity, self-determination, authenticity, and resilience (Turner et al., 2022).

Summary

The strength of faith, whether religiously or spiritually based among Black men, is a driving force in their resilience when facing the myriad stressors and challenges in their lives as Black men. Spirituality and religion's historical and traditional nature are woven intricately into the very fabric of Black men's lives and their families, churches, and communities. Psychological research has demonstrated that spirituality and religion build resilience in all individuals, and research studies have shown the crucial role that spirituality and religion play in the lives of Black men. The Black church is central to the lives of Black men and their families, and it creates an extension of the family that provides support and an environment where Black men are exposed to role models who have high levels of resilience. Those relationships help Black men navigate the difficulties they face in life. The spirituality among African Americans has historically, and still in the present, built resilience among Black men. Although some research shows that the number of Black men attending church has fallen, the reality is that there are still many Black men involved in their churches and faith communities. Most research shows that Black men engaged in the Black church draw upon a source of love, support, and relationships that help them build the needed strength and resilience to cope with daily issues. One factor that stands out, not only in this chapter but also in the entire book, is the need for Black men to have mentors to assist them in overcoming the barriers they face. Mentoring supports Black men in navigating life's difficulties and provides them with the experience and wisdom of older, more experienced Black men. The following chapter will discuss the dynamics of romantic relationships and friendships for Black men and the impact of societal pressures and personal growth on relationships.

Chapter Eleven

Love and Relationships

In this book, various aspects of Black men's lives have been examined thus far, diving deep into the factors that affect Black men and their functioning in society and the community. However, this chapter discusses the dynamics of romantic relationships and friendships for Black men, including the impact of societal pressures and personal growth on relationships. Research indicates that Black men are less likely to marry than their White counterparts (Rice et al., 2023). Black men cope with the stressors of racism, discrimination, stigma, and stereotyping that impact them psychologically and affect their ability to maintain long-term relationships. Furthermore, the conceptualizations of Black men about what it means to be masculine may conflict with relationship-forming, both in terms of romantic relationships and friendships. These issues will be examined to discover how men can overcome these challenges and build strong, healthy relationships.

The Impact of the Perception of Masculinity on Black Men and Their Relationships

Research has shown that the idea of masculinity is inherently linked to the sexual identity of Black men (Crook et al., 2009). Masculinity is defined as "a socially constructed set of hierarchical relations among and between men" (Crook et al., 2009, p. 361). However, masculinity among Black men has been defined as "an emphasis on physical strength, an expectation of submissiveness and strength in women, angry and impulsive behavior, functional (and often violent) relationships between men and between men and women, strong male bonding" (Franklin, 1984, pp. 60-61 cited in Harris, 1995, p. 280). Black men are socialized into their masculinities by four specific groups, including family, peers, the military, and pop culture. However, Black men are also socialized via their church community. From a social constructivist view, masculine attitudes and behaviors are "learned and produced in social institutions and reinforced through human actions" (Crook et al., 2009, p. 361).

Furthermore, racial identity and masculinity are linked by similarities in the process of maturity and development in the reference group in the lives of Black men (Crook et al., 2009). That reference group, an inherent source of the culture of masculinity, is one that the individual adheres to psychologically and forms the individual's attitudes, values, and norms (Crook et al., 2009). There is an expectation that Black men will conform to the dominant culture's views of gender roles; however, it is a challenge for Black men to blend their culture with the dominant culture (Crook et al., 2009). Black men often believe they must project themselves as tough or express a 'cool pose,' which can negatively impact their ability to build relationships. The stigma attached to Black men often overlooks other expressions of masculinity, including the roles of protector, disciplinarian, and provider (Crook et al., 2009; Rice et al., 2023).

Challenges to Forming and Sustaining Romantic Relationships

Various factors impact the ability of Black men to form lasting romantic relationships, including developmental factors, such as coming from a single-parent home or having experienced abuse from a parent as a child (Kogan et al., 2016). Racial discrimination and harsh parenting affect Black men's ability to sustain romantic relationships (Kogan et al., 2016; Rice et al., 2023). However, the socioeconomic circumstances of Black men may work to undermine their relationships (Kogan et al., 2016; Rice et al., 2023). The majority of research that has been conducted on Black men and romantic relationships has tended to examine issues such as public health issues like the risk for HIV and teenage fatherhood rather than reviewing the developmental processes that affect Black men's ability to form lasting romantic relationships (Kogan et al., 2016).

However, Kogan et al. (2016) undertook such a study, hypothesizing that when Black men are exposed to negative and harsh parenting as children, their commitment behaviors are impacted via effects on emotional regulation, specifically in terms of how anger manifests. The study stated a belief, based on previous research, that lack of warmth in the family resulted in an outcome of chronic anger, impairing the ability of Black men to form relationships and express themselves positively toward their romantic partners. The study was undertaken with 315 Black males. Black male youth and their parents were interviewed. The study found that Black males who experienced harsh parenting held significant anger, and the experiences of racism and poverty contributed to the anger. The study concluded that:

"During the emerging adult years, involvement in high quality, committed relationships signals the development of psychosocial maturity and the ability to engage in intimate relationships… [however], "for African American men growing up in socioeconomically disadvantaged environments, low levels of relationship commitment may forecast low involvement with enduring marriages" (Kogan et al., 2016, p. 11).

The reality for Black men is that they often begin their lives with experiences that make them angry, suspicious, and untrustful of the world around them. As they are impacted by negative parenting and family situations, with the added burdens of discrimination and poverty, they do not have the foundation necessary to build healthy romantic relationships. It does not help that pop culture is portraying masculinity in such negative ways, but without a solid foundation, too many Black men grasp onto those in the pop culture as role models for what it means to be a man.

In a recent study that examined romantic relationships among Black men, Bae and Kogan (2020) examined how the quality of Black men's romantic relationships changes over time. Aligning with Kogan (2016), Bae and Kogan (2020) noted that challenging and stressful experiences and environments undermine relationship quality and stability for Black men. Stressful experiences and events in life can discourage Black men from investing effort and time into their relationships and partners. The focus of the study was to examine how support, trust, and relationship conflict influence Black men's views of their relationships (Bae & Kogan, 2020). It was hypothesized that adversity during childhood, community disadvantage, and socioeconomic woes would be linked with the quality of romantic relationships in the lives of Black men (Bae & Kogan, 2020). The findings were surprising, since 50 percent of the Black men in the study revealed that they have well-functioning and supportive relationships despite their life challenges (Bae & Kogan, 2020). The study found that positive relationship development among Black men is common, indicating that resilience mechanisms exist to support positive outcomes (Bae & Kogan, 2020).

Despite positive outcomes presented by Bae and Kogan (2020), other research has indicated that the younger generation of Black men, particularly the millennial generation, has experienced barriers to forming romantic relationships due to socioeconomic circumstances—leaving men in that generation still living in their parent's homes (Jackson, 2020). However, that is not to say that Black men view marriage as any less important than previous generations; it is viewed as a healthy goal in adulthood. Previous research has indicated that healthy relationships among African Americans are characterized as:

"egalitarian relationships as partnerships that include a shared division of labor, commitment to investing in the larger African American community, interdependence, and collective career and family aspirations," countering the patriarchal views where the wife is seen as the extension of their spouse" (Jackson, 2020, p. 2).

However, that does not mean that Black men always resist the sexist and racial stereotypes of how they are portrayed. The influence of media propaganda that portrays Black men negatively may be internalized, creating problems in romantic relationships or even the ability to form those relationships— particularly the way that pop culture, stigma, and stereotyping portray those men (Jackson, 2020). When all those factors combine, it is not surprising that Black men have difficulties in forming healthy and lasting romantic relationships.

Jackson (2020) conducted a study to examine Black men's views on romantic and casual relationships. The participants revealed that partnership is vital in romantic relationships and supported by self-development. The Black men emphasized flexibility and personal growth, indicating that a prerequisite for healthy relationships was personal mental, emotional, and physical health. One participant revealed that a past failed relationship could be attributed to his lack of healthy self-development and stated:

"...and that's where it goes back to having that relationship with God; it's imperative because if you don't know who you are, because at that time I would struggle with my identity. If you are not healthy mentally, and you don't have those standards, those morals, those principles, and you don't stand your ground and set your expectations up front, the relationship will set it for you" (Jackson, 2020, p. 26).

That participant's statement reveals how foundational the church may be in the lives of Black men to supporting their ability to develop healthy relationships. Many of the study's participants revealed that romantic relationship problems arose from past unresolved trauma from their family in childhood (Jackson, 2020). Another participant revealed this about ensuring their personal health to support a romantic relationship:

"I'm learning that it is very important. I didn't think it was important until I got in one [relationship]. After that, I felt it was important to be aware of your mental health, but I didn't realize how important it was or how valuable therapy could be. I personally haven't gotten therapy yet, but I plan to, because I'm realizing that there are things that I need to work out as a human and also to be better for somebody else. And I think a lot of us do realize that" (Jackson, 2020, p. 28).

The participants also revealed an understanding of flexibility in romantic relationships and the need to be emotionally available, revealed in one participant's statement:

"Yeah. Again, I think it's [about being] emotionally available based on what the two partners agree upon. I'm a huge proponent of people being who they are, and they should express themselves how they want to express themselves, and that looks different for every relationship. So maybe early on in the relationship, you may not need to be that emotionally available because you've only known the person for a short period of time… but I think maybe as the relationship grows and develops, you establish what level of intimacy needs to be there from an emotional standpoint" (Jackson, 2020, p. 30).

Another participant revealed the flexibility in romantic relationships and negated the need for gender scripts in the following statement:

"We're [not] living in this 1900s dynamic where a man has to do this, the man has to be the head of the household, the man has to supply – or the woman stays and cooks and nurtures the children. And then one thing we have to come to understand is it's like a different time. I don't mind providing. However, I know she's not going to want to stay home and do that. And I'm not forcing the issue on her because like, I want her to achieve her dreams too. So yeah, I think societal demands come into the role. People expect you to do this and perform a certain way when it comes to the patriarchy of the household. Whatever. It's a different time" (Jackson, 2020, p. 32).

That statement highlighted the general sentiments of the Black men in the study, who indicated that they had no desire to burden their partners with societal expectations. The participants also revealed an understanding of communication's role in romantic relationships and the integral need for trust. One participant revealed:

"I know a few people who are my age and married, but I want to break that curse of Black men not being able to be family men, they can't be faithful, they can't be good fathers. I want to be the father that they never had. So, I just want to break a lot of generational curses and show the world what Black men are capable of" (Jackson, 2020, p. 39).

The Black men in this study understood what it takes to form healthy romantic relationships (Jackson, 2020). However, many Black men do not have the foundation of a role model to follow in their lives and romantic relationships, and far too often, the stigmatization of Black men—further reinforced by pop culture and combined with socioeconomic disparities—steers them in the direction of unhealthy relationships due to their lack of mental and emotional health. However, the participants in Jackson's (2020) study deeply understood what it means to form healthy relationships, and the research showed that when Black men are emotionally and mentally healthy, they are more likely to form long-term romantic relationships. The findings in Jackson's (2020) study align with other research in this book about the need for Black men to develop robust mental and emotional health to function successfully.

Moreover, research has shown that when Black men are in relationships with Black women who share the same cultural understandings and experiences of discrimination, it provides a psychosocial resource in the functioning of the relationship (Rice et al., 2023). The shared knowledge of the tribulations and trials faced in the Black culture creates intimacy in the shared burden of racism (Rice et al., 2023). When Black males are in long-term romantic relationships, they can draw upon mental and emotional support, and those relationships offer opportunities for affirmation when faced with racism-related stressors (Rice et al., 2023). One study examined the reasons that Black men married and found that five specific factors encouraged them to marry, including the characteristics of their wife, spirituality, a desire to be together in a relationship with their wife, being ready for marriage, and receiving encouragement from others to marry (Hurt, 2014). The barriers to marriage among Black men were cited as a perception of the loss of freedom, previous experiences with relationships, disapproval from those they knew, and their personally held reservations (Hurt, 2014).

Social exchange theory helps explain the decisions to marry among Black men because it holds that self-interest is the primary motivation to understand people's actions when making relationship decisions by balancing the costs and rewards (Hurt, 2014). Despite the support available for Black men in committed romantic relationships, the lack of a positive male role model may stand in the way of their relationship resilience. Although no studies were identified concerning older Black males mentoring younger Black males about their romantic relationships, mentoring as a benefit to Black men has run throughout the tapestry of this book and would offer considerable benefits to younger Black men who experience discrimination, racism, stigma, and wish to rise above the stereotypes and pop culture that seek to define them.

Black Men and Friendships

Friendships play a crucial role in an individual's life, influencing their activities, their worldview, and the way they relate to others (Ríos-González et al., 2021;

Taylor et al., 2024). In the case of men, the traditional gender norms and roles might limit the development and benefits of developing close relationships with other males. Often, Black men form toxic male friendships that exert pressure on them to participate in habits that are not healthy, including alcohol and drug abuse. Psychological stressors, such as gender stereotyping, influence the ability of men to join healthy friendships despite the benefits of friendship in their lives (Ríos-González et al., 2021). However, friendships have been linked to positive psychological and mental health and well-being (Taylor et al., 2023). Having friends has been shown in research to relate to fewer symptoms of depression and negative psychological stress (Taylor et al., 2024). Research has indicated that friendships are also linked to high self-esteem and happiness (Nguyen et al., 2016; Taylor et al., 2024).

It was challenging to find many reports on Black men and their development of friendships, which was also noted by Taylor et al. (2024), who revealed that a shortage of studies exists in this area of inquiry. Therefore, Taylor et al. (2024) conducted a study to examine the friendship support networks among African Americans. Although the study is not specific to Black men, it does offer pertinent information about friendships among Black men and within their community. It followed social exchange theoretical underpinnings that investigated the relationships between individuals and their romantic partners, family members, community, and religious organizations based on the critical nature of reciprocity in social exchanges. In other words, reciprocal relationships involve a healthy flow of giving and receiving social support. The study collected data from interviews with African Americans and discovered that involvement in close relationships and friendships offers social support and emotional engagement. Married individuals are less engaged in social networks. Still, those who are single are more likely to seek social support from others outside their family, indicating that friendships are a high priority among all African Americans, including Black men. The study concluded that the friendship support networks among African Americans include reciprocal support (Taylor et al., 2024).

However, some research reveals that Black men have difficulties forming friendships with other Black men. Gilchrist (2006) stated, "I think this issue is a silent crisis that is crippling Black men and our ability to forge meaningful relationships with each other while also seriously undermining our coping skills as life presents constant challenges" (para. 1). Gilchrist (2006) explains that he does not have five close male friends to call on if he needed to and blames the machismo culture among Black men. He explains that men have spent too much time and resources on "the quest for women" but believes that Black men can share their fears, dreams, and hopes with one another (Gilchrist, 2006). Black men are generally more comfortable expressing their emotions to women but cite the incredible opportunity to build strength and resilience among Black men if they form close relationships with one another and provide support (Gilchrist, 2006). The research proposes that counseling and mentors are essential for Black men who struggle with their masculine identity and, unfortunately, adhere to the stereotypes that exist. Counseling would help them overcome the challenges associated with a negative Black male identity (Harris, 1995). Counseling and mentors can assist Black men in channeling their anger and negative self-perceptions in a safe environment and help them construct a positive identity that allows them to embrace a feeling of self-efficacy in their endeavors, including in relationship-building.

This sentiment is shared by a young Black man who attends Ohio State University, Emmanuel Addae Aweah, who noted that Black men are accustomed to internalizing everything due to the challenging roles they are required to fill in society in a landscape characterized by stereotypes and stigma. Aweah (2023) shared how, as he developed his true identity, he was shunned by the world and understood that all Black men experience the same. However, Aweah stated the following about Black men developing relationships:

"As we build this sense of community and foster it between us, we have control over how the media depicts us; although the media can say whatever it wants, if we're in a community together, where we witness positivity in those who look like us, that is what you're going to remember. Us as black men, we rarely get to experience intimacy from each other, the moments where we can break down the wall without fear of the next man, women, or individual using it to suppress you. A lot of us walk around with so much baggage up in our mind, that we would love to unload and just feel relief from just for a moment; but our identity is so tied to having to showcase just being a 'man' 24/7 and whatever stereotypes come with that (Aweah, 2023, para. 6).

Aweah (2023) also cited the need for Black men to embrace mental health services when needed to overcome stressors and help them build a solid and healthy identity.

Summary

This chapter has examined the dynamics of romantic relationships and friendships and how societal pressures and personal growth impact relationships. Societal pressures harm Black men in their conceptualization of what constitutes masculinity, as they often fall into the trap of adhering to the stereotypes portrayed about them in the media and within pop culture or of following negative parenting role models. The emphasis on physical strength and the attempt to appear 'cool' to others often limits Black men from forming romantic relationships. Black men are socialized through their peers and family, as well as pop culture, and for those who are in the military, the emphasis on strength is further accentuated. However, the learned behaviors of Black men may be more positive, particularly for those raised in two-parent families, in stable homes, and who are involved in the church and the tight-knit Black community where everyone is viewed as part of an extended family, although in some cases that may be a negative influence, depending on their geographical location.

Stressors in the lives of Black men also impact their romantic relationships. Stressors include socioeconomic difficulties, racism, and discrimination, which contribute to the Black man's formation of a negative identity. However, Black men who form strong and lasting romantic relationships often have a partner who can help them cope with those stressors, providing a refuge of understanding and compassion. Younger Black men, particularly millennials, were shown in the study to understand that personal development is crucial to ensuring good romantic relationships. However, the problem that exists is the lack of role models for many Black men who may have grown up in a home with harsh parenting. As a result, they carry those negative feelings into their romantic relationships. The information in this chapter reveals the need for Black men to develop positive mental and emotional health to support their success in romantic relationships.

Although friendships play an essential role in any individual's life, influencing how they view the world, relate to others, and determine many activities they participate in, the gender norms of Black men may limit the development of solid friendships. When Black men do not have good influences via friendships in their lives, they may become involved in harmful activities, forming bad habits. Gender stereotyping may also affect the ability of Black men to form strong friendships. Since friendships are linked to better psychological well-being, Black men must form friendship support networks. Friendships help Black men avoid internalizing their struggles and provide a community where they can come together and overcome the negative stereotypes about them. Mentoring and counseling offer great hope to assist Black men in developing a positive self-identity. The following chapter will delve deeper into the importance of community involvement and support networks and provide examples of community leaders and organizations making a difference.

Chapter Twelve

Community Engagement

This book has examined many aspects of the lives of Black men that affect their existence and functioning in the world, looking at various issues of systemic racism and discrimination, mental health effects, and how Black men can overcome the multiple problems in the workplace and educational settings. The book has also examined the relationships in the lives of Black men and the struggles they experience in forming lasting romantic relationships and friendships. Additionally, it has briefly touched upon the importance of community engagement for Black men. However, this chapter will examine the importance of community involvement and support networks for Black men while providing examples of community leaders and organizations making a difference.

Black Males and Community Involvement: Challenges and Barriers

Research has shown that Black males' community involvement and civic engagement result in positive social and personal outcomes (Smith et al., 2022). Various forms of community involvement exist among Black males, including church participation. When Black males are involved in the Black church, they participate in religious practices as well as social and political activism. While family, friends, and neighborhoods help create a positive and supportive system, for many Black males, particularly those in urban areas, negative factors impact their development. After-school programs in urban areas have been shown to support social networks, allow Black male youth to learn from older, more experienced men in their community, and provide information about how they can make a difference in their communities. Research has examined how Black males perceive limitations in the community and the resources that exist. It has been noted that when Black males have positive experiences with various teachers, peers, the Black church, and other programs linked to the school, they have positive outcomes in their decision-making. Mentors are particularly critical for Black males (Smith et al., 2022).

A study was conducted using the African American Male Theory (AAMT) to examine the developmental opportunities for young Black males in after-school programs specific to mentoring and interpersonal relationships (Smith et al., 2022). The principles of the AAMT theory include a focus on individual experiences alongside the collective experiences of Black males, the uniqueness of being a Black male, the continuity of the African culture in terms of how biology and consciousness influence the experiences of Black males, the resistance and resilience of Black males, and how race and racism combined with sexism and classism, affect every aspect of the lives of Black males, with a focus on research-based programs. The factors identified that present barriers to community involvement among Black males include mistrust, lack of confidence, individual perceptions, and financial constraints. In urban areas, Black male participation in community programs is also affected by systemic racism (Smith et al., 2022).

It is noted that programs to engage Black males in the community must "acknowledge the complexities of family and social society" to provide a structure that assists Black males in their development; in other words, programs and activities must be culturally appropriate (Smith et al., 2022, p. 15). The study examined the involvement of Black male youth in the high school setting and their attitudes and perceptions toward participation in a 4-H program. The study revealed that nearly one-half of the participants described the condition of their community as only 'average.' Problematic is the finding that many young Black males do not perceive community involvement as necessary. However, the participants in the 4-H program cited community involvement as essential, indicating the need for Black male youth to be involved early in such initiatives (Smith et al., 2022).

Research has noted that the strength and success of the Black community are highly dependent on the well-being of Black men (Hyman, 2006). Within the Black community are community and family support systems, described as:

"The immediate ecological environments whose resources are used to provide the nurturing, norms, and networks needed for a positive racial orientation. Also, important is the values orientation of men with respect to their cultural practices and spiritual beliefs. These values are the lenses that help men define who they are in relationship to the larger world – i.e., their responsibilities both to themselves and for others – and they provide a framework that helps to guide choices and distinguish one's views of right and wrong" (Hyman, 2006, p. 11).

The assumption is that the more positive the Black male's personal makeup, the more likely he will contribute positively to the community. However, the opposite may also be true when he has negative personal characteristics (Hyman, 2006). Therefore, any interventions must have a specific focus on ensuring the positive aspects of character and competence are enhanced among Black males. However, this is not simple for Black males or their communities due to the structural forces that exist at a national and institutional level and have erected barriers to their ability to develop those positive attributes that influence how Black men perform in the world. The outcome, when Black men face such barriers, is that they do not possess the power needed, or when they do, they do not know how to use it. Geographical advantages also exist due to what is termed as "de facto segregation," creating political, economic, and race-based disadvantages (Hyman, 2006, p. 12). Therefore, focusing on positive youth development among Black males is critical (Hyman, 2006). Hyman (2006) noted that recruiting mentors in the Black community requires spreading the word via word-of-mouth, using marketing materials, such as flyers and posters, and contacting local leaders to recruit participants. Ensuring that community organizations are involved is essential, and the media can be used to generate the needed support for the program and assist in recruiting mentors. Using the internet, newsletters, and community events helps with recruitment efforts. The focus is to build a community of mentors to support Black men in becoming more involved, building strength in their lives, and preparing them to mentor the next generation (Hyman, 2006).

Initiatives, Models, and Leadership Examples to Increase Black Male Community Involvement

Taylor (2023) revealed four organizations highly committed to supporting Black men, including 100 Black Men of America, Black Men United (BMU), the Black Male Voter Project, and Black Men Teach. Black Men United is described as a national community service organization focusing on restoring and rebuilding Black communities. BMU is under Black male leadership (Black Men United, 2024). The mission of Black Men United is to create an alliance of Black men to lead communities in spirituality, safety, and economics, focusing on returning pride to Black families and building bridges within the community (Black Men United, 2024). The Black Male Voter Project focuses on increasing civic engagement among Black men and supporting them to take their rightful place in the world and influence it with their participation (Black Male Voter Project, 2024). Black Men Teach is an initiative focused on increasing the number of Black male teachers in the educational environment in Minnesota (Black Men Teach, 2024). Black Men Teach aims to build up Black male teachers, engage them in a fellowship, and build a strategic framework of collaboration by recruiting, preparing, placing, and retaining Black men in teaching positions. These types of initiatives are vital within Black communities and bolster Black men's engagement and involvement.

The 100 Black Men of America, Inc. initiative has been previously mentioned in this book and involves scholarship and mentoring programs for young Black men to ensure they can realize their best potential (100 Black Men of America, Inc., 2024). When young Black men achieve their best potential, they can engage in addressing the national and local issues that impact their communities (100 Black Men of America, Inc., 2024). 100 Black Men embraces the understanding that not all Black youth can access a positive network or opportunities. Those involved in the 100 Black Men Initiative are focused on committing themselves to displaying the types of individuals that children will not only look up to, but will also emulate, ultimately providing Black youth with a choice rather than being relegated to the brokenness that exists in many Black communities. There are currently 100 chapters in the United States, and the organization has existed for 57 years with a proven model. The motto of the 100 Black Men initiative is "What they see is what they'll be" (Medium, 2021, para. 3). This motto drives the motivation for its members and highlights the responsibility they hold toward those they mentor and their communities (100 Black Men of America, Inc., 2024).

100 Black Men executive board members Phillip Barnett and Marco Lindsey revealed that they became acquainted with the program via mentorship (Medium, 2021). According to Chuck Baker, the Chairman of 100 Black Men in the Bay Area, "Our mission is to improve the quality of life within the Bay Area and beyond by advancing the social, economic, health, and educational progress of African Americans" (Medium, 2021, para. 2). Baker also stated,

"With over 60% of Black youth growing up in single-family households, often led by women, the role of the 100 Black Men could not be more critical. Our motto is, 'What they see is what they'll be.' We ultimately want to provide young Black men with people to look up to, who will support them, and who will not just be present, but have a meaningful and positive presence in their lives" (Medium, 2021, para. 3).

Marco stated the following concerning 100 Black Men:

"I realized early in my career that mentorship and a support system would help me advance greatly. So, I began looking for organizations to get involved with that would help me give back and provide me with a community of like-minded individuals" (Medium, 2021, para. 4).

Marco works with 100 Black men in the marketing and public relations areas and launched a 2016 initiative that helps community members with networks and other activities when they are interested in a tech career (Medium, 2021). According to Phillip, he became involved as a university student. Phillip connected with Black men on the 100 Black Men board and started the collegiate mentorship program. Phillip revealed, "My experience with the Collegiate 100 gave me insights into what 100 Black Men does as an organization and created a pathway for me to become a member" (Medium, 2021, para. 7). Through his work training and developing young Black men to take their place as community leaders, he became aware of and part of the 100 Black Men initiative (Medium, 2021). Phillip noted that it is impossible for a Black man to thrive unless the community is also thriving, so partnerships with various organizations and actors in the community are necessary to support Black men undergirded by mentoring relationships.

Mentoring Black Males to Become Actively Engaged in Their Communities

It has already been emphasized throughout this book that mentoring for Black males is incredibly important. However, the study has not yet examined the specific benefits of mentoring. At this juncture, a further examination of mentoring is warranted. Everyone has "a birthright to be all that we can be. Mentors are those special people in our lives who, through their deeds and work, help us to move toward fulfilling that potential" (Green-Powell, 2012, p. 99). Whether it is community mentoring, educational mentoring, workplace mentoring, religious mentoring, or any other type, mentors help individuals rise above their perceived limitations. Mentoring is defined as "when a role model, or mentor, offers support to another person. A mentor has knowledge and experience in an area and shares it with the person being mentored" (Green-Powell, 2012, p. 99). Mentoring also involves the investment of time by the mentor in the mentee to help that individual grow. The systemic racism and discrimination that Black men face often make them feel as if it is of no use trying to combat those barriers to achievement in various areas of their lives. However, mentors can assist them in navigating difficulties by sharing their experiences and knowledge (Green-Powell, 2012).

While mentoring is valuable for the mentee, there are also rewards realized by mentors as they watch the person grow and develop a unique friendship and bond with the mentee (Green-Powell, 2012). Just as mentors assist individuals in realizing gains in their workplace status, help them with better educational achievement, and help them develop more spirituality in the religious setting, mentors are critical in the community setting to help Black men embrace their place and role in the community.

Mentoring also increases mentors' leadership skills and allows them to bring impactful change to the lives of the mentees and their communities, particularly salient in the lives of Black men. Mentors help the mentees set goals and achieve them, assist them in confronting negative attitudes and behaviors, and listen and teach by example. Mentors provide wise counsel, help trigger self-awareness, and inspire the mentees' lives (Green-Powell, 2012).

The United Way of Greater Philadelphia and Southern New Jersey understands the importance of mentoring Black male youth and has developed a guide to procuring mentors (Grimes, 2014). The organization reveals the importance of mentoring to assist young Black males in achieving in school and notes that youth mentoring has the benefits of socialization, especially for Black males who are not effectively prepared and trained, who have limited networks and connections to adult Black male role models, and who lack the needed skills and ability to function effectively in education and society. The community-led focus on Black males' development is considered critically important. Two types of mentoring are noted as particularly vital for Black males, including (1) instrumental mentoring, which is problem-focused to help them overcome barriers and achieve their goals, and (2) psychosocial mentoring, which helps Black males change their attitudes and behaviors that negatively impact their outcomes. Mentoring is shown to reduce depression and develop more positive beliefs, with an outcome of being more accepted by their peers. Although the United Way's initiative is educationally focused, these forms of mentoring can assist Black men in developing the skills, behaviors, and attitudes that prepare them for more involvement in their communities and the potential to effectuate community change, ultimately preparing them to be the next generation of mentors for younger generations (Grimes, 2014).

In my doctoral dissertation, I examined how spiritual formation and soul care in the Black church impacted the church's involvement in the community. The findings from the study indicated that the church plays an integral role within the community, which means the church is a central organization in the lives of Black men that can prepare them to become more effectively involved in the community. One of the research's primary findings was that church mentorship is vital to preparing Black men to fulfill their roles as active community members.

Mentoring is important because organizations within the Black community, including Black churches, can provide mentors to assist Black men in fulfilling their potential to engage in and positively impact their communities. The information previously revealed in the book emphasized the importance of the Black church in the lives of Black men. Developing a solid spiritual foundation for Black men requires that they are prepared to fulfill their God-given roles in the world around them successfully. Spiritual preparation and effective mentoring are critical to ensuring Black men are actively engaged in their communities and prepared to build consensus networks and influence the policies and laws affecting their lives.

Starting Early in the Lives of Black Males is Vital

As already indicated by the information reviewed about various Black male initiatives among youth, beginning early in the lives of Black males is critical to ensure they are prepared for community involvement. However, research has shown that Black males lack the needed social support within their communities and schools from an early age (Phillips et al., 2018). Adolescence is a particularly tough age for all children. Still, among Black male youth, the environment and stressors impact them more negatively, mainly due to the conditions of neighborhoods, problems in the family, neighborhood violence, and poor socioeconomic conditions. It is during adolescence that young Black males develop severe high-risk behaviors due to cognitive, biological, and social changes that occur during those years of development. Focus group studies were conducted among Black males aged 11 to 14 and their parents (Phillips et al., 2018). The negative effect on Black males in their community was cited as including limited resources and funding (Phillips et al., 2018). One participant revealed,

"We can't afford art programs for the children or music programs. My son, for instance, is good at drawing but so far, getting him into an art program, without really me pulling out a lot of money out of my pocket, I can't do it. Therefore, it's just a wasted talent, which a lot of these children are very talented" (Phillips et al., 2018, p. 84).

The parent participants revealed a need for positive reinforcement and ongoing engagement among Black male youth in the educational setting (Phillips et al., 2018). This study revealed the need for interventions targeting young Black males in the school and community setting to provide support and ensure a positive trajectory. The study noted the need to begin early with young Black males and use a holistic approach to support them in realizing their full potential (Phillips et al., 2018). The 100 Black Men of America, Inc. initiative demonstrates how the negative trajectory of young Black males can be changed by providing them with mentors and a support network. It is not enough to say that we should focus on involving Black men in the community. Instead, community involvement among Black males must begin early in life to prepare them with the knowledge, education, and skills to contribute positively to their community. Evidenced by the benefits of the 4H program among Black youth, initiatives must begin early to instill in Black men the importance of and their ability to be active stakeholders and players in community initiatives that benefit their lives and the lives of others in the community.

Research has indicated that to further the economic and social growth in Black communities, Black men are a vital resource for collective action (Farmer, 2006). However, the breakdowns in Black men's community involvement have not been well-researched, but stressors and incarceration are cited as partially responsible. A study was undertaken to understand how those specific factors have affected Black males' prosocial community involvement. It is acknowledged that the civic engagement framework helps to understand Black men's problems for community involvement at the micro, macro, and mezzo levels. For example, at the micro level, the personal characteristics of Black men are based on their economic status, educational level, and commitment to their community, which all serve as positive or negative community resources. Black men who have good health, are married, and are younger have a higher likelihood of participating in their communities' civic life via providing funding to non-profit organizations and volunteering than Black males with socioeconomic struggles and those who are older (Farmer, 2006).

Outcome expectancy is another micro-level factor pertaining to whether Black men see potential positive outcomes (Farmer, 2006). At the macro level, factors such as the Black church supporting Black male involvement in their community and their willingness to help address social problems. Participation in any faith-based organization is predictive of community involvement among Black males. Mezzo-level factors include the trust that Black males have for others in the community, but social exclusion, racism, and discrimination can inhibit Black males from community involvement. However, when trust is built between others in the community and Black men, they are more likely to become involved in the community. Institutional and organizational distrust may dampen Black men's community involvement. Sixteen organizations were involved in the study in 41 communities in the United States. Interviews were conducted among 1,500 participants. The study found that:

"Consistent with findings in previous research... there is no simple relationship between forms of social capital and civic engagement; [however,] positive outcome expectancy, diversity of one's social network, and social capital are all positively associated with African American males' civic engagement" (Farmer, 2006, p. 66).

Building more diversity in Black males' social networks is recommended to increase their trust in organizations and institutions and support a growth in community involvement (Farmer, 2006). The acknowledgment of the need for Black men to develop diverse social ties within their network further supports the idea that interventions should begin early in the lives of Black males to help them build friendships and connections that last across their lifespan. This enables them to be more effective community members due to a more extensive social network to draw on in cooperation and collaboration to benefit their communities.

Summary

Black men are a critical resource in their communities if they are actively involved in addressing the problems that are experienced among African Americans, especially among Black male youth. Mass incarceration of Black men and poor socioeconomic status have plagued Black men for decades. However, Black churches and initiatives such as the 100 Black Men of America have acknowledged the need to prepare young Black males early to take their place as critical actors in their community. The formation of mentoring programs to assist Black men in overcoming the micro-, macro-, and mezzo-level factors that affect their ability to be a positive resource in their community has been shown to help youth develop positively and have a better life trajectory. While mentoring has been an essential factor in every area of Black men's lives examined in this book, the information in this chapter emphasizes its importance, beginning early in the lives of young Black males. The following chapter will discuss the role of art, music, literature, and other creative outlets in expressing and healing Black male experiences. Included will be the profiles of influential Black male artists and their contributions.

Chapter Thirteen

Artistic Expressions

The previous chapters in this study have examined various areas in the lives of Black men that affect their functioning in an environment characterized by systemic racism and discrimination and their resilience to overcome. Relationships have been examined, and how Black men function most effectively has been reviewed. This book also examines Black men's mental, physical, and spiritual health needs. However, it would be remiss not to explore the role of art, music, literature, and other creative outlets in expressing and healing Black male experiences. This book chapter will examine those issues and present profiles of influential Black male artists and their contributions.

Art Forms in the African American Culture

The Black population has used many forms of artistic expression to present its world experience and highlight the struggles linked to race. One example of that type of creative expression is found in the poetry of Tupac Shakur, who wrote:

"You wouldn't ask why the rose that grew from the concrete had damaged petals. On the contrary, we would all celebrate its tenacity. We would all love its will to reach the sun. Well, we are the rose – this is the concrete – and these are my damaged petals. Don't ask me why, thank God… ask me how!" (Tupac Shakur, 2000 in *The Rose that Grew from Concrete,* cited in Griffith & Semlow, 2020, p. 373).

In his poetry, Tupac Shukar expresses the struggles of a Black man in today's world, but he also relates the resilience that exists in coping with those struggles. According to Griffith and Semlow (2020), art is "part of antiracism organizing" because, through art, it is possible to bring about changes in awareness of the existing cultural differences while promoting personal healing, reducing prejudice, and supporting individual transformation and growth (p. 375). Art may take many forms in this endeavor, including music, film, poetry, painting, and others. Artistic expression builds an awareness of oppression and promotes healing among those with this experience, supporting self-actualization.

One of African Americans' most significant art forms is the musical form found in the spirituals (Brown, 2013). When African Americans converted during slavery to Christianity, the religion was reshaped to meet their unique needs, and Christian beliefs were blended with traditional African beliefs. The spirituals were songs that drew from the stories in the Bible and were based on themes of hope, salvation, and freedom while expressing deep sorrow over living in bondage and hope for a better life to come.

Frederick Douglass stated the following of the spirituals:

"They would sing words which to many would seem unmeaning jargon but which nevertheless were full of meaning to themselves. I have sometimes thought that the mere hearing of those songs would do more to impress some minds with the horrible character of slavery than the reading of whole volumes of philosophy. I did not, when a slave, understand the deep meaning of those songs. They told a tale of woe which was then altogether beyond my feeble comprehension; they were tones loud, long, and deep; they breathed the prayer and complaint of souls boiling over with the bitterest anguish. Every tone was a testimony against slavery and a prayer to God for deliverance from chains... Slaves sing most when they are unhappy. The songs of the slave represent the sorrows of his heart; and he is relieved of them, only as an aching heart is relieved by its tears" (Brown, 2013, p. 54).

African Americans, including writers such as Phillis Wheatley, a late 18th-century author, have produced much literature (Brown, 2013). In the 19th century, slave narratives dominated African American literature. However, by the 1920s Harlem Renaissance, African American writers were widely recognized, and Toni Morrison won the Nobel Prize. The themes contained within African American literature included their experiences with racism, incorporating aspects of the culture, equality, and slavery, and included oral forms such as sermons, spirituals, blues, gospel music, and rap.

By the 20th century, works written by Booker T. Washington and W. E. B. Du Bois were published in nonfiction form that confronted the racist attitudes of the time. Other writers included those during the Civil Rights movement, such as Gwendolyn Brooks and Richard Wright, who focused on Black nationalism and racial segregation. African American literature has founded itself firmly in the world of literature with books such as Alex Haley's *Roots: The Saga of an American Family,* and Alice Walker's, *The Color Purple* (Brown, 2013).

The oral poetry of the African American culture is evident in sermons that use cadence, deliberate repetition, and alliteration (Brown, 2013). The culture of African Americans is quite distinct from the general American culture, although it is also intricately interwoven into the culture. However, African American culture is a blend of Sahelean and Sub-Saharan African cultures, impacted by the experience of slavery and the interaction with other cultures in the United States, including the Native Americans. The outcome is a dynamic and unique culture that profoundly impacts the mainstream culture of America (Brown, 2013).

The inability to receive an education among Black slaves meant they could not read or write, so their first stories were passed through oral traditions and included folk tales such as John Henry. Through the African American oral tradition legacy, an impact continues as Black preachers speak and perform using emotion along with dance, song, and verse, often a feature of the sermon, all influenced by early oral traditions among African Americans (Brown, 2013).

Also, aspects of the African American oral tradition are rhyming, trash talk, wordplay, and semantic inversion, which have become integrated into the popular culture of America, as well as having "become internal phenomena" referred to as "spoken word artistry" (Brown, 2013, p. 58,59). During the 1960s and 1970s, the Black Power movement gave rise to popular Black recording artists such as The Impressions and Nina Simone.

During the 20th century, African American music progressed to Broadway, infiltrating rock and roll, while soul and R&B developed, becoming music genres that White audiences embraced. However, it is not just music and literature that have affected the mainstream American culture, as African American painters and artists and their creative works have become valued throughout the United States, from the art forms of quilts and wrought-iron and ceramics to the landscapes that were produced in the decades of the 1960s and 70s. Contemporary African American artists of note, such as Charles Tolliver, demonstrate how African American art forms have influenced American society (Brown, 2013).

Art Forms and Resilience

Music is the most often researched art form related to promoting healing (Stuckey & Nobel, 2010). Music has been demonstrated in research to reduce anxiety and create emotional balance, supported by the science that shows that music helps "restore effective functioning in the immune system partly via the actions of the amygdala and hypothalamus" (Stuckey & Nobel, 2010, p. 255). However, the visual arts have also been explored in healing. It is reported that art assists individuals in expressing things they have experienced that are far too difficult to talk about and allows them to explore the meanings in their lives. Research has shown that people use artistic expressions to construct a positive identity and make sense of their experiences. Previous studies have shown that creative expression helps in expressing grief, improving well-being, reducing negative emotions, creating more positive emotions, and reducing depression and even physical illness symptoms. The belief that creative expression contributes powerfully to the process of healing has been embraced across many diverse cultures (Stuckey & Nobel, 2010).

According to one Black artist:

"Like many Black families, music and dance were an integral part of my upbringing, and it was my way of connecting with others in the community. I felt the essence of music deep within me when I played both jazz and European classical music, learning from Black teachers. What I have found is that through these creative collaborations, I am able to freely express my Blackness. Being Black in the United States comes with societal messages of inferiority, stereotypes, and generational trauma. Finding freedom in music and dance has been liberating for me" (Martin, 2022, p. 72).

That realization led Martin (2022) to conduct a study to examine the experiences of other Black artists and how involvement in music and the arts helped Black Americans build resilience. Martin (2022) noted how little research exists concerning African Americans and music therapy, making the study important. The participants for the study were from Pittsburgh, Pennsylvania, and were asked to collaboratively improvise on the theme of being African American in the United States. The participants' responses to the experience of improvisation based on their experiences yielded the interplay of emotions, sensations, memories, images, thoughts, and the inter- and intrapersonal interactions and dynamics experienced by the participants. Semi-structured interviews were conducted with the participants, and one of the primary themes was resilience or "making a way out of no way... finding new ways to express ourselves" (Martin, 2022, p. 84).

Also noted as part of the resilience that arises from various artistic forms of expression among the Black participants was joy, pride, and freedom. Artistic forms such as music and dance were also found in the study to have allowed the participants to express their spirituality, such as a spiritual connection, healing, the sacred, and honoring their ancestors. Overall, musical and artistic expression enabled the participants to experience historical connections, collaboration, and interconnectedness with the world around them. The theme of Black Power was identified in the participants' responses, which were related directly to healing and uncovering the roots of racism and exposing it by sharing it. Specifically, "the role that Black musical and cultural experiences or lifeworlds played in the collaboration was significant and an integral part of understanding how the participants described their Blackness (individually and collectively), embraced it, and expressed their pain." (Martin, 2022, p. 87).

Art Forms that Promote Healing

According to West (2022), today's Black music, particularly Hip Hop, reflects the African American culture in terms of the pain and suffering of Black people. West (2022) revealed that rappers reveal the truth, even when it hurts them personally. Hip-hop highlights mental health issues, and Black artists take on the responsibility of speaking for their culture and the pressure that exists in overcoming personal battles. Black artists discuss addiction, trauma, societal oppression, and anger and motivate those listening to not give in to the pain, which is vital since therapy is so stigmatized among Black men. Music is therapy for those creating it and those listening as it resonates with their struggles. From the traditional spirituals to more contemporary expressions in music, the theme of hope and victory runs deep. Rapper Lecrae provides positive messages in his music about faith and belief in healing (West, 2022).

One example of a Black male artist who uses his art forms to promote healing in the Black community is Archie Green (Copeland, 2022). Green founded an organization, 'Peel Dem Layers Back,' to promote mental health advocacy using rap while bringing awareness of the stigma associated with mental health problems and treatment access in Black communities (Copeland, 2022). In his most recent song entitled 'Too Many Funerals,' he expressed that too many African Americans are dying from mental health issues (Copeland, 2022). Green stated,

"As far as mental health is concerned, in the Black community, we need to talk more about this. And using rap is a powerful tool. Hip-hop is what makes things cool, and so I was like, I want to make mental health cool" (Copeland, 2022, para. 16).

From the spirituals of slavery to the popular music of today, Black artists have utilized music as a source of power and strength to encourage one another to continue the fight for freedom (Green, 2024). Green notes the spiritual that developed post-slavery titled 'Oh Freedom' and its lyrics that declared hope and held up the song 'Freedom' by Beyonce with the lyrics "Hey! I'ma keep running, cause a winner don't quit on themselves" (Green, 2024, para. 3). Black music through songs helps to promote strength and resilience and helps Black individuals break through the chains of oppression and systemic racism.

The Association for the Study of African American Life and History (ASALH) examined arts and African Americans. It revealed that "Black music emerges as a critical art form that assists in pushing toward equity and justice for all" (Green, 2024, para. 5).

Music and artistic expression help African Americans in general, and Black men in particular, to build a positive racial-ethnic identity characterized by resilience in an environment of racial injustice (Turner et al., 2022). Active expression supports Black men in engaging with the world in ways that help them demonstrate their agency, authenticity, self-determination, efficacy, empowerment, and innovation. This may take the forms of storytelling, dance, poetry, theater, visual arts, or other activities as they celebrate and express joy, humor, and courage. Those types of "vehicles for expression can counter the suppression of emotion, silencing, and invisibility of racism-related experience. Amplifying cultural narratives and sharing the truth of lived experiences enhance processes of voice and visibility" (Turner et al., 2022, p. 558).

According to Turner et al. (2022), "for Black men, musical expression such as Hip Hop has been found to be a healing, strengths-based, culturally congruent vehicle for emotional wholeness, connection-building, healing grief, and resisting oppression" (p, 558). Consider Tupac's lyrics in the song entitled *Dear Mama,* and specifically in the second verse, which says:

"Now, ain't nobody tell us it was fair.

No love for my daddy, 'cause the coward wasn't there.

He passed away and I didn't cry.

'Cause my anger wouldn't let me feel for a stranger (Genius.com, N. D.).

Tupac goes on to reveal in his lyrics about slinging drugs and seeing his mother in the kitchen working with scraps to make "miracles every Thanksgivin," and in this song, he details the struggles of so many young Black boys as they grow up without a role model and father figure. However, in the last verse of his song, Tupac states the line, "If you can make it through the night, there's a brighter day, everything will be alright if you hold on. It's a struggle every day, gotta roll on" encouraging those listening to his music to keep the faith for a better day (Genius.com, N.D.).

The lyrics of many Hip Hop artists contain intelligent creativity and have the capacity to present a five-minute summary and do it poetically (Jenkins, 2011). The primary aspects of Hip Hop music:

"Align with the Black male experience in America – poor health, negative interactions with the criminal justice system, love for family, social oppression, violence, social rage and frustration, community leadership and activism, depression, prison industry complex, enslavement, unemployment, poverty, and the need for communal and self love" (Jenkins, 2011, p. 15).

The Black male music artists of today address those social ills. While many think hip-hop is only centered on violence, drugs, money, and women, music artists such as Jay-Z have displayed high levels of intelligence that have not been recognized. When Jay-Z appeared *on The Oprah Winfrey Show*, a video introduction focused on the most traditional way that success and manhood are defined in the United States; however, in his article published in *O Magazine* and his interview with Oprah, his community experience, talent, and intelligence were highlighted. Jay-Z spoke about his writing of songs and how those have been a central element in highlighting the severe political problems and social issues Black men face. Jay-Z revealed that his *Gangster* Album, when listened to in progression, tells a story about the "rise and fall of a hustler. And within each song, the artist displays his mastery of lyrical style and content" (Jenkins, 2022, p. 15).

According to Jenkins (2011), the reason that today's Hip-Hop artists possess such a free platform for speech can be accredited to the Harlem Renaissance artists who set the foundation for passion, creative energy, and courage needed to share their thoughts and continue to critique, reflect, and navigate, via art, the class and racial based experiences of Black men in America. Hip-hop contains worth because it is "truth expressed through a politic of imagination and creativity" (Jenkins, 2011, p. 17).

Today's rap music may positively impact Black men; for example, consider Kendrick Lamar's album *Good Kid, M.A.A.D. City,* which is a story about his journey to escape the bad influences in his life and how they kept pulling him back (Wilson, 2018). In the song *The Art of Peer Pressure,* he relates how he committed a home invasion when he was young with his '*homies.*' The word '*homies*' is interwoven throughout the song, and he talks about how he only drinks and smokes dope when he is with them. He says, "Really, I'm a sober soul, but I'm with the homies right now" (Wilson, 2018, p. 6). This song reveals an experience that other Black males can relate to, as the song expresses Lamar's personal experience and offers alternatives to drug use and violence. The song says, "No better picture to paint than me walkin' from bible study… I don't mind 'cause one day you'll respect the good kid" (Wilson, 2018, p. 6). The message in the song is to persevere in being a good kid even when trapped inside a mad city. Black males' experiences in the cities are described in such detail that they can seek solace in the song and understand they are not alone in the experience. Using his songs, Kendrick Lamar is a positive role model (Wilson, 2018).

Before Hip-Hop and Rap became central in the landscape of the Black music genre, Rhythms and Blues (R&B) songs were used by artists to express their feelings about the world around them and the experiences they had with the world (Chaney & Mincey, 2014). R&B was a softer genre of music that allowed free expression of experiences and feelings and allowed the artists to show sensitivity. One study examined the themes contained within the song lyrics of both R&B and Hip-Hop and found that in those types of music, sensitivity was expressed in four different ways: (1) private sensitivity, (2) partnered sensitivity, (3) perception sensitivity, and (4) public sensitivity. Just as it sounds, private sensitivity was the expression of feelings that Black men have when they are alone and hide their feelings from others. Partnered sensitivity occurs in romantic relationships or relationships with friends and the community. Perceptive sensitivity was when men felt for the sorrows of others, acknowledging that in society, they must suppress their emotions. Public sensitivity involved Black men crying out publicly and expressing how they do not care about what others think about them. Each of these themes offers the profoundly personal experiences of Black men in the world around them (Chaney & Mincey, 2014).

The Science of Music on Healing

According to Bieber (2023), "Music is an untapped resource when it comes to the healing arts" (p. 1). Writings on music's role in the individual's life and in balancing them are tracked back to ancient Chinese and Greek philosophers. For example, Plato expressed the critical nature of music in combination with personal development, physical development, and education. Plato held that music provides nourishment to the soul, and the connections between music and the listener have the power to keep them on a noble and righteous path. Music can also provide a sense of purpose and meaning and establishes a link between the individual's "conscious and unconscious mind, but also between man and the divine" (Bieber, 2023, p. 2).

Bieber (2023), has been a researcher in music for three decades after receiving a Master's in Music, undertook a research study with seven participants to examine the impact of music on the listener. After listening to music, the participants were interviewed, and several themes were identified in their responses. The first theme was that music works to quiet the mind. Music was found to stabilize the participants and clear their minds, allowing them to feel more grounded and transcendent. The participants expressed that the music was calm and healing, especially for the 528 Hz track, which contained two known healing frequencies. The participants revealed how their frustrations fell away, and their minds felt clear. The participants also indicated that music created a heightened awareness that extended outside of themselves into the world around them. The music was also found to produce sensations of warmth and to distract the participants from their problems (Bieber, 2023).

Recent research has indicated that sound can be used in healing, referred to as sound meditation or healing (Goldsby et al., 2022). However, the research in this area of inquiry is still lacking, although it has a long history. In Tibet, the use of singing bowls has been shown in research to reduce heart rate and blood pressure, while quartz singing bowls have been used among cancer patients, each showing promise. Mitchell Gaynor, a famously known oncologist, has reported Singing Bowl sound healing to help cancer patients with healing. The science of sound and music healing is based on the knowledge that an electrical or energy field surrounds the human body and that sound waves can interact with and change the field. Research holds that the vagus nerve might be stimulated when sound healing is used to bring about feelings of well-being, as indicated in a vibrational study of music. A study examined the phenomenon, and participants were asked to answer questionnaires after receiving sound healing. The intervention consisted of Tibetan singing bowls of various materials. The participants reported changes in depression, tension, anxiety, and notably in faith and spirituality after the intervention (Goldsby et al., 2022).

Summary

Recent scientific discoveries and research reveal what African Americans knew long ago – music is healing. Music and artistic endeavors help release the sufferings of individuals and allow them to connect with the spiritual and divine. Music helps Black men talk about their struggles and shines a light on their hope and resilience even in the face of systemic racism and discrimination. The spirituals helped Black slaves cope with their situation, look to God for hope, and have faith in better times. That same strain of thought continues in today's Black music as the evils of society are revealed but overcome by the ideas of hope and faith. The following chapter will examine the involvement of Black men in political movements and advocacy and the impact of activism on personal and community healing.

Chapter Fourteen

Political Activism and Social Change

This book has examined various aspects of Black men's lives and how systemic racism, discrimination, and stigma affect them and their resilience to overcome. This chapter will discuss the involvement of Black men in political movements and advocacy and how activism impacts personal and community healing. First, the history of political activism and social change will be examined, followed by a review of Black men, activism, healing, and how personal healing impacts community healing.

History of Political Activism and Social Change

Political activism and social change have a long history among African Americans in the United States. Understandably, political activism and a drive toward social change are deeply rooted in the Black culture due to their experiences with the evils of slavery and ongoing systemic racism, discrimination, stigma, and inequalities in various areas of the lives of Black people. The history of activism among Black men in the United States goes far back to the Underground Railroad (N'Guessan, 2022). The Underground Railroad was formed during slavery as a system to assist slaves hoping to escape to freedom (N'Guessan, 2022). Slavery was a system that completely subjugated the Black man to the power of the White man, a system of debasement and dehumanization against which many Black men fought to seek freedom (N'Guessan, 2022). One such man was Frederick Douglass (1818–1895), an activist and statesman, although he was born into slavery in a rural area of Maryland (Sandefur, 2020). Frederick Douglass experienced the ills of slavery. However, when he turned 20 years of age, he escaped slavery via the Underground Railroad and went to Massachusetts where he became involved in the abolition movement (Sandefur, 2020). Douglass was also an author and lecturer, and he used his writing talent to publish *The Narrative of the Life of Frederick Douglass, an American Slave* (Sandefur, 2020). Douglass continued as an activist during the Civil War, recruiting Black soldiers to fight in the Union Army (Sandefur, 2020). Douglass was well-acquainted with Abraham Lincoln and, following the Civil War, was appointed to the position of minister to Haiti (Sandefur, 2020). Douglass continued his activism by promoting civil rights and speaking against Jim Crow laws and practices during the period following Reconstruction (Sandefur, 2020).

The story of Frederick Douglass relates the evils of slavery and his experience. Through his publication, he actively brought awareness to the practice and moved the nation toward ridding itself of slavery (Sandefur, 2020). Frederick Douglass was inspired by William Lloyd Garrison, who led one wing of the abolitionist movement. However, Douglass questioned Garrison's theories and began working with a different wing of the movement that believed the Constitution was not a document that supported slavery, differing from Garrison, who thought it was radically pro-slavery. It was Douglass who argued that enslaved individuals were American citizens and that Black men were part of all men declared to be created equal. Frederick Douglass's arguments considerably impacted the issue and the progress of the abolition movement. Douglass emphatically opposed any racial separation doctrine, holding that all Americans have a shared destiny and a common inheritance in the principles of the Declaration of Independence and the U.S. Constitution (Sandefur, 2020). Frederick Douglass stated,

"My mission is to plead the cause of the colored millions of our countrymen against injustice, oppression, meanness, cruelty, and to hasten the day when the principles of liberty and humanity expressed in the Declaration of Independence and the Constitution of the United States shall be the law and the practice of every section, and of all the people of this great country without regard to race, sex, color, or religion" (Sandefur, 2020, p. 35).

Activism during the Civil Rights Movement between the 1950s and 1970s was led by the Reverend Martin Luther King, Jr., a Black man and preacher. During the middle part of the 1950s, racial and ethnic discrimination and separation were present (Wang, 2023). Although the 14th and 15th Amendments guaranteed equal rights and the right to vote for African Americans, those constitutional protections were not sufficient. Segregation was evident in the states where African Americans were given what was termed "separate but equal" facilities (Wang, 2023, p. 2263). At this time, Martin Luther King, Jr. entered the scene and established the Southern Christian Leadership Conference (SCLC) to assist institutions in the South with civil liberties. Martin Luther King, Jr. led the Civil Rights movement, encouraging African Americans to express their dissatisfaction with the status quo using nonviolent expressions, such as voter registration drives and sit-ins. However, in 1963, King and those following him were arrested in Birmingham, Alabama. It was from the Birmingham Jail that King wrote his letter, which is famously known as the *Letter from Birmingham Jail*. King's alignment with nonviolence in protests assisted him and his followers in fighting effectively against discrimination and bias (Wang, 2023).

Following his having been arrested and placed in jail, later in August 1963, King planned another event and, at the Lincoln Memorial, delivered his speech "*I Have a Dream*" (Wang, 2023). This march had a significant impact, leading to the passage of the Civil Rights Act in 1964. However, King's path was not easy; in his 1965 campaign focused on registering Black voters that took place in Selma, Alabama, the march turned into a situation where the state police used tear gas and batons. This march turned so violent that it is now referred to as "Bloody Sunday." Just two days later, King led a second march, and he told those he was leading to kneel submissively and pray, choosing a peaceful option. Although he lost some of his support by choosing peace, in 1965, the Voting Rights Act was passed. However, King was involved in other activism in the social sphere to promote human welfare, including voicing concerns about the nuclear conflict. The Civil Rights Movement led by Martin Luther King, Jr. changed the face of the nation and helped Black Americans win the rights that had been denied to them for centuries in the United States (Wang, 2023).

However, failing to mention the Black church and pastors' role in the Civil Rights Movement would be remiss. The Black churches are central to the lives of African Americans, and this was true during the Civil Rights struggle with, as already mentioned, the Southern Christian Leadership Conference (SCLC) playing a huge role in the movement and accompanied by the Congress of Racial Equality (CORE) and the Student Nonviolent

Coordinating Committee (SNCC) (Ghose, 2019). However, without the support of the Black church, neither King nor those leadership conferences would have made the difference they did. It is held that "In this sense, the Black church can be regarded as the mother organization that not only shaped the organizations involved but also engaged the leaders who came to lead the Civil Rights Movement in different phases" (Ghose, 2019, p. 59). Furthermore, history shows that the Black church represented the institutional center for the civil rights movement. The creed of the Civil Rights Movement was nonviolence and based on the belief that God does not sanction oppression. Hence, the church teachings helped connect the purpose of the movement to the spiritual Christian teachings, which were symbolic of the African American culture. Therefore, the Black church set a legacy for activism for social change through peaceful means (Ghose, 2019).

A more recent example of social activism among African Americans is the Black Lives Matter (BLM) movement; however, it has not gained the same support from the Black church as the Civil Rights Movement, and there is no representation of clergy in the movement because it is viewed as too militant and disruptive, and it is cited as being far too secular and removed from Christian principles (Napierala, 2021). However, that does not mean that activism is dead among Black men. As I wrote in my Doctor of Ministry dissertation, activism often extends from the Black church. Black churches are organized around making a difference in their communities through their teachings and community outreach work to bring about social change. In my church and several other Black churches, we implemented a spiritual development and soul care program to prepare our congregants to develop a deeper relationship with God, which ultimately resulted in them reaching out to the community. The Black church has historically played the role of activism center, as evidenced by the Civil Rights Movement led by Martin Luther King, Jr. James Cone described liberation theology as one of the primary schools of thought within the Black church (Avent & Cashwell, 2015). According to that theology, Black Americans adapted Christianity to the problems and triumphs they experienced (Avent & Cashwell, 2015).

The Black church has historically been a place where Black Americans could gather and talk about their problems and a central location to create and enact change on a community level (Avent & Cashwell, 2015). However, the Black church has also been viewed as an alternate society, one that is sovereign, enabling African Americans to express themselves authentically (Avent & Cashwell, 2015). What is certain is that the Black church is the nerve center for activism that effectuates social change, as Black churches have intricate ties with Black colleges and universities and other activist organizations in the African American community. The role that faith-based organizations such as churches play in underserved communities cannot be understated (Owens et al., 2020). In the earlier days of the church, the communalism of African Americans was combined with Christianity. Still, the Black church worked to build information-sharing networks and share resources throughout an extended family network (Owens et al., 2020). The same is true today for the Black church, and wherever there is advocacy for African American men, one can be confident that the Black church is, to some extent, involved. There are some criticisms of the Black church's involvement in activism; for example, it is held that when the Black church defines its purpose based on the cultural agenda, it risks focusing on social change more than making disciples (Jones, 2011). However, to some extent, I disagree because just as Martin Luther King, Jr. insisted on peaceful protests against the conditions of discrimination and inequality, the Black church should be the voice of reason in any social activism efforts to ensure that nonviolence is the approach used to bring about change.

Black Men, Activism, and Healing

Research has been conducted to examine the impact that activism toward social injustices and bringing about social change has on African Americans and has noted that frequently, those injustices may "provoke Black rage, but this emotion must be channeled toward constructive goals rather than self-destruction" (Roberts, 2023, p. 15). The last decade has been highlighted by many protests and social justice movements among African Americans, with research documenting the adverse impact of racism on mental health that is experienced due to social inequalities and discrimination.

Despite those impacts, African Americans have displayed resistance and resilience in the face of trauma by drawing on their community and cultural resources to promote their well-being and healing. Research also shows that when African Americans have an activist orientation toward engaging in social, political, and collective movements to address disadvantages or injustices, they have a creative outlet that leads to higher well-being (Roberts, 2023).

However, the same effect is not noted when engaging in activism characterized by high-risk or those that are more disruptive or confrontational (Roberts, 2023). High-risk activism may lead to adverse outcomes, such as PTSD (Roberts, 2023). However, conventional activism involving the more mainstream and legal forms of participation is more likely to result in positive outcomes than high-risk methods. A study was undertaken following the Black Lives Matter movement, and the Black Community Engagement Survey was used to recruit participants. A total of 400 participants were involved in the study. Several measures were used, including the Activism Orientation Scale (AOS), the PTSD Checklist, and the Ryff Scales of Psychological

Well-Being (Roberts, 2023). The study found that African Americans engaged in the community and those who are spiritually engaged and activists reported higher levels of psychological well-being (Roberts, 2023). However, among males involved in high-risk activism, PTSD symptoms were higher, but those involved in conventional activism had a decrease in symptoms of PTSD. It is noted that:

"These favorable outcomes associated with conventional activism orientation are consistent with the strategies employed by anti-racist activities to resist oppression. These strategies encompass a comprehensive understanding of self within social, political, and historical contexts, engaging in critical actions for power and liberation, and practicing critical self-reflection" (Roberts, 2023, p. 23).

Furthermore, when activism is grounded in liberation and wellness, it has the positive effect of helping resist racial oppression while also resulting in more positive personal outcomes, including higher levels of life satisfaction and self-esteem (Roberts, 2023).

In a separate study that examined the role that social activism plays in the lives of African Americans following their exposure to media coverage relating to police brutality, Alexander et al. (2022) recruited participants for a two-year longitudinal study. More than 2,300 individuals were screened for the study, but the final number of participants was 304 African American adults. The study was undertaken following the death of George Floyd, who died while in police custody in 2020, in the city of Minneapolis, Minnesota. The death of George Floyd made a significant impact in the United States, and many demonstrations and protests occurred. Although some of the protests were characterized by violence, causing millions in damage, 95 percent of the protests were not violent. Research has shown that when individuals engage in activism, it helps them address their feelings of vulnerability and express traumatic experiences through social engagement (Alexander et al., 2023).

Alexander et al. (2023) held that social activism may serve as a mediator and moderator in mental health, so they sought to test that idea. The participants' engagement in social activism following the George Floyd riots was measured using Pew Research items. For example, the participants were asked about their engagement in specific activities, including (1) contacting public officials, (2) contributing financially to an organization or group that focused on racial issues, (3) attending rallies or protests, (4) discussing the issues with friends or family, or (5) sharing content on social media concerning racial equality. The study found that the participants who did engage in those activities had better mental health perceptions than those who did not engage in social activism. Conceptualizing social activism as a moderator in the study revealed that when inundated with media representations of police brutality against African Americans, the failure to participate in any type of social activism predicted worse mental health. However, those with higher levels of activism following media representations of violence against African Americans were found to have better mental health perceptions. The study indicated that even actions as small as discussing social issues with friends and family can lead to better mental health in the face of racial issues (Alexander et al., 2023).

One study examined how activism among Black student leaders on one campus assisted in effectuating social change at a predominantly White institution and noted that the Black Lives Matter social movement is an organizational platform that activists use to protest against anti-Blackness practices in institutions and society (Hotchkins, 2017). The movement is described as a transgenerational model that supports the ability of Black individuals to access equal rights. Black students attending predominantly White institutions frequently become engaged in social change movements and join Black organizations, allowing them to play leadership roles and conduct activist activities in the cyber realm and the community. It is noted that the support for Black students to become leaders at predominantly White institutions is supported by parents who have socialized their children about the vital role of participating in activist activities and contributing to Black communities by becoming involved in organizations (Hotchkins, 2017).

The study reported by Hotchkins (2017) was conducted among African American students, seven of whom were men and four of whom were women, to understand how transgenerational knowledge is applied by Black student leaders in pursuing social change at a predominantly White university. Following the interviews, the theme of "preserving my Black" was identified, and participants revealed having been racially socialized to possess self-worth and high cultural esteem. The participants expressed the understanding that history would repeat itself if they were not focused on pursuing interventions for themselves and other Black students. One participant noted that their parents hold expectations that they will challenge systems of oppression such as inequity and racism and gave advice about how to organize sit-ins and conduct other activities to gain attention to the problem. Another theme identified in the participants' responses was a "digital underground" or activism via social media and the ability to reach others with accurate information, gain a consensus, provide encouragement, and organize around issues. For example, one participant revealed:

"When Mike Brown was murdered, the media flooded the airwaves with images of him giving the finger so they could frame him as deviant, which means deserving of dying violently. In response, his family circulated the picture of him in the graduation cap and gown. We used the #IfIDieUseThisPic campaign to show us [Black students] as non-threatening, prosperous members of our college community so they [White folk] can understand that we also contribute to society in positive ways" (Hotchkins, 2017, p. 276).

The findings in the study concluded that activism in its various forms assisted the participants in developing a healthy identity through their interpersonal interactions and racial resistance. They were able to disrupt marginalization, oppression, and racism while creating solidarity among themselves and ultimately developing leadership abilities and effectuating social change throughout their school community (Hotchkins, 2017). The Pew Research Center has noted in a survey conducted among African Americans that social media is used widely in activism to reach larger groups and build consensus around issues affecting African Americans (Auxier, 2020). From posting to support causes, encouraging others to take action, and locating rallies, African Americans use social media frequently for activism (Auxier, 2020).

A stellar example of an African American man who used social activism to address a serious issue and found his own healing was Edwin "Eddie" Ellis (1941-2014) (Turner, 2022). Ellis served as an advocate and community activist for those formerly incarcerated after being sent to prison to serve 25 years for a crime he did not commit. During his incarceration, Ellis earned multiple degrees and became involved in the Think Tank organization formed by those incarcerated. The organization discovered that among those incarcerated in New York State, they were all from just seven neighborhoods. Upon his release, Ellis gave classes in those neighborhoods to address the ongoing cycle of incarceration and ultimately worked with the Governor of New York State and other officials. Ellis founded the Center for NuLeadership on Human Justice & Healing to assist those leaving prison with gaining employment. From a former Black Panther to a community activist, Ellis made a real difference in the lives of Black men and their communities and found his healing from his experience of incarceration despite his innocence (Turner, 2022).

Summary

Political activism toward initiating social change is not an add-on in African Americans' lives and communities but an integral part of their existence. From the days of slavery to the contemporary ills of systemic racism, discrimination, and inequality, political activism has, at its core, the struggle of African Americans to change their experiences and existence in the world around them. Overcoming the rage felt by African American men at the inequalities, discrimination, racism, and stigma they feel in the world, political activism allows them to work to make meaningful changes in their lives and communities. The research in this chapter has revealed how political activism toward social change helps Black men form a healthy identity and realize life satisfaction and well-being, knowing they are making a difference for themselves, their families, and their communities. Seminal examples of Black male activists such as Frederick Douglass and Martin Luther King, Jr. demonstrated how, through peaceful activism, enormous societal changes can be realized. The peaceful forms of political activism and social protest are a model that contemporary political and social activists have followed to make substantial changes for the Black population. Community-building and collective action are key for Black men in building strong and healthy identities and developing the capacity to change their lives and the lives of those in their community. The following chapter will synthesize the themes and insights from the previous chapters in this book and offer practical strategies for collective healing, including recommendations for therapy, community initiatives, and policy changes.

Chapter Fifteen

Pathways to Healing

This chapter is the final chapter of this book and explores the many struggles that Black men face in their lives. It synthesizes the themes and insights from the previous chapters, offering practical strategies for individual and collective healing, including therapy, community initiatives, and policy recommendations.

The Struggles of Black Men

The historical trauma suffered by Black men has created a tenuous situation as they struggle to find meaning in their lives in the dominant culture of the United States (Burrowes, 2017; Halloran, 2018). Even though slavery ended long ago, the ongoing experiences of systemic racism, discrimination, stigma, inequality in opportunities, and socioeconomic struggles continue to impact the lives of Black men (Burrowes, 2017; Pough, 2019). Predominantly Black neighborhoods are characterized by poverty and poor infrastructure in homes, city buildings, and schools, making Black men and their families feel as if they are less than others and not worthy of the equal treatment afforded to most Americans (Logan, 2013; Pough, 2019; Scott-Jones & Kamara, 2020; Wilson, 2023).

Black males grow up in homes without fathers due to the mass incarceration of Black men and often lack the necessary role models to support their success.

Black men further experience health disparities, particularly in the areas of their mental and physical health, which are both negatively impacted by inequalities and stigma (Joseph et al., 2024; Ugwuede, 2023). The mortality rate among Black men in the United States is exceptionally high, driven by mental health issues and poor physical health. However, there are excellent examples of Black men who have overcome the struggles that are collectively experienced by Black men, such as Ben Carson and the entrepreneurs presented in the book. However, Black men need someone in their lives who positively influences their self-perception if they are going to rise above their struggles. Among the many factors revealed in this book to impact Black men positively is the effect of having close connections with other Black men who offer encouragement and support.

Societal stereotypes weigh heavily on the minds of Black men and affect their perception of their abilities, particularly in educational and occupational settings (Harris & Kruger, 2022; Melson-Silimon et al., 2023). This book has revealed how social identity theory—arising from the experiences and feelings of Black men about belonging to a social group—affects their self-perception (Buckley, 2018). Often, when Black men excel in college or their careers, they are beset with what is known as imposter syndrome and feel as if they do not belong (Chakraverty, 2020; Cokely et al., 2024). The sources of anxiety and stress for Black men in today's world are many, and they struggle to overcome the stress associated with their race and gender. Cultural pride is vital in assisting Black men with embracing who they are and building the strength to overcome stereotypes (Bannon et al., 2009; Brown, 2013; Johnson & Carter, 2020).

Black men also struggle with their understanding of masculinity or the belief that they must be tough and strong—a concept further driven by the music industry, which places value on money, drugs, and women rather than the family structure that is so vital in the lives of Black men (Scott-Jones & Kamara, 2020; Teti et al., 2012). Struggling with a faulty conception of what constitutes masculinity leaves Black men attempting to survive and thrive without the benefit of other Black men who can offer them guidance. The toughness that Black men feel they must portray also interferes with their relationships with their partners and children, causing family breakdown and dysfunction. When combined with their other struggles, this complexity makes forming relationships even more challenging, and many do not consider the benefit of accessing any mental health services or counseling (Bae & Kogan, 2020; Kogan et al., 2016; Rice et al., 2023). However, when Black men develop healthy relationships with their partners, they tend to be more mentally and emotionally resilient and have better outcomes (Hurt, 2014; Rice et al., 2023)

Starting Early: Interventions in the Lives of Young Black Males

Research shows that interventions during the early years of education for Black males are essential. However, research in this area is lacking. The studies that have been conducted indicate that Black boys experience problems associated with gender and race at very young ages (Wint et al., 2022). Although the family is a protective factor, this is not the case for all young Black males, who need role models—such as successful Black men—to guide them (Bell, 2019; Collins, 2022; Sánchez, 2016).

As early as preschool, Black males experience a system that is prejudiced against them and face a high rate of expulsion in their early school years. Black males also tend to receive harsher punishments and have their competence questioned due to the lack of Black teachers who are not culturally competent. Black boys in school are often treated as older than they actually are by teachers who do not understand their behavior. The outcome is that Black boys are expelled from school or suspended at higher rates than their peers.

The findings show a critical need for Black role models in the lives of Black boys from an early age. Research presented in this book has indicated that school-based mentoring programs are crucial for Black boys, ensuring they have Black male mentors they can trust within the educational system (Sánchez, 2016). Black mentors help young Black boys stay in school and perform well instead of dropping out, joining gangs, and becoming involved in criminal activities (Collins, 2022; Ross, 2017).

Black males need mentors throughout their education (Bell, 2019; Collins, 2022; Cummings, 2019; John, 2024; Ross, 2017; Sánchez, 2016; Smith, 2023; Watson, 2024).

Mentors and Role Models Across the Lifespan

Throughout the entirety of the book, in every area examined, having a mentor to guide them assists Black men in fulfilling their roles as students, husbands, fathers, and members of the community (Bell, 2019; Collins, 2022; Cummings, 2019; Cozart, 2016; Harris & Kruger, 2022; Sánchez, 2016; Ross, 2017; Thomas, 2024; Watson, 2024).

Of the various programs reviewed in the book, including the Manhood Development Program, having a role model and mentor was powerful in assisting Black men with self-actualization and successfully navigating multiple aspects of their lives (Givens et al., 2016).

Mentors and role models are essential to help Black men overcome the ideas of masculinity that are deeply ingrained in their culture so they can direct their lives in a way that allows them to form deep and abiding relationships with others rather than being swept along with the status quo of Black male masculinity in the mainstream society.

The Young Men, Masculinities, and Mental Health (YBMen) project was reviewed, which assisted Black men and boys in challenging rigid gender roles, enabling them to have more social interaction and redefine manhood (Watkins, 2019). Notably, the need to understand how gender, race, and other factors intersect is crucial when approaching Black men with any intervention to support them.

Another model reviewed was the Black Love, Activism, and Community (BLAC) model, which points

Black men toward the development of caring relationships and love for God to assist them in living authentically, exhibiting caring and compassion, self-determination, and interconnectedness with the community (Turner et al., 2022). The BLAC model focuses on community and communality based on a spiritually centered existence. Black men need relationships with other Black men to build resilience and an environment of support, particularly in mentor and mentee relationships where Black men can build one another up, and older Black men can serve as role models for younger Black men.

Mentoring has a long history and is evident in the Bible. Contemporary research has shown that mentoring assists Black men in growing, changing their self-perceptions, and accomplishing things they could not have done without that support. Black men need help in every area of their lives, from receiving encouragement to seeking mental health services to finding support and assistance in being good fathers and husbands.

These types of support are significant for Black men who have been incarcerated as they reintegrate into their homes and communities because incarceration has set them behind in achieving what they could have achieved.

Community-building through mentors and role models can assist Black men in developing the connections they need to find work after release so they can contribute positively to their families and communities.

As a central source of support in the Black community, the Black church should be involved in, if not lead, such efforts. A grassroots effort is needed to develop programs that will help Black men overcome the problems associated with incarceration and successfully return to the community.

Initiatives exist, such as the 100 Black Men of America, Inc., that empower Black men by focusing on improving the lives of Black communities and enhancing their education and opportunities. More initiatives like this are needed to assist Black men.

However, the workplace is often characterized by discrimination against Black men, and the information in this book has revealed that building professional networks can assist them in overcoming those problems and help them thrive (Hawkins, 2022; Palmer, 2008; Strayhorn & Johnson, 2020).

Building professional networks requires making social connections both in the workplace and in the community, so Black men can consult with mentors to assist them in overcoming the issues they face in the workplace.

In all areas of struggle experienced by Black men, the information in this book has revealed that mentors are essential. Social support networks are critical for Black men in the community, church, educational settings, or workplace. However, social support networks must be successfully constructed, and mentors play a vital role in enabling Black men to build those networks.

Black Churches: Reaching Out to Build Spirituality in the Black Community

The research in this book has revealed the central importance of spirituality and religion in the lives of Black men and the role that religious coping plays in well-being (Chung et al., 2014; English, 2016; Park et al., 2017). The

Black church's role in Black men's lives cannot be overstated, particularly in helping them develop resilience (Lincoln & Mamiya, 1990; Salinas et al., 2018; Tate, 2023).

The Black church helps Black men develop a positive identity, providing a place of refuge, access to role models, and an extended family. Cultural resources shared within the Black church offer its members a sense of affiliation, helping them flourish through the social networks they develop in the church and the broader community.

The Black church's vital role in Black men's lives makes it a critical aspect of their resilience and healing. Therefore, the Black church must be involved in any initiative to help Black men on their path to healing and strength because it already contains the necessary ingredients and experience to support them.

The Need to Promote Therapy

As the information in this book has revealed, Black men suffer from PTSD, depression, and other mental health disorders at an increased rate due to their life experiences. Problems also exist with substance abuse disorders, which often co-occur with mental disorders. However, due to structural racism and biases, Black men may delay seeking treatment for mental health disorders, causing more serious clinical outcomes. Black men who live in urban, low-income areas are at an increased risk of exposure to violence. The experiences of Black men that impact their mental health extend to incarceration. In this environment, they may lose their sense of self, and once they return home, they cannot function effectively within their families and communities.

There is a need to address the barriers to mental healthcare access for Black men, and particularly the stigma associated with receiving help. Black men generally hold a negative set of attitudes and beliefs toward accessing mental healthcare services because therapy is not an accepted practice among most Black men or African Americans in general. Black men also tend to turn to spirituality and religion when facing mental health issues, making it essential that Black churches and pastors develop connections with mental health providers in the community so they can refer Black men to them for therapy.

There is a need to drive awareness among the African American population about the necessity and acceptability of accessing mental healthcare services and to increase awareness about the availability of those services. If African Americans are more aware of the need for services, it is more likely that the family members, friends, and other people in the lives of Black men will encourage them to seek help when needed. Research shows that when Black churches are involved in promoting mental health services, Black men are more likely to seek those services. When Black churches partner with other organizations to raise awareness, a more positive narrative about help-seeking can be created in the Black community and among Black men. Policymakers should focus on ensuring that funding is available to assist Black men in receiving mental health services while they are incarcerated so they can better function once they return to their homes and communities.

Community Partnership and Mentorship Programs

The starting point for addressing the problems experienced by Black men in all areas of their lives is the development of community mentorship programs. Community programs should be developed by local Black churches and other organizations that help Black men connect with others in the community. As the research in this book has shown, building social connections is key to advancing Black men in all areas of their lives. A tight-knit network of Black men at the local community level has the power to support Black men in developing strong marital and family relationships by serving as role models who demonstrate what is required to have a successful marriage. Building social networks at the community level will also help Black men in tapping into the community resources that will support their employment and success. As older Black men mentor younger Black men, strength will grow in local communities, enabling Black men to realize success in all areas of their lives.

Community mentorship programs and meetings can highlight mental health services and service providers who can be asked to speak to the group, building trust among Black men in seeking mental health services when needed. The importance of building a group of Black male leaders in each community is central to Black men overcoming their barriers to effective functioning and success. There is power in numbers, and as Black men form coalitions with one another, they will understand that they are not alone in the struggle. Ultimately, the entire fabric of communities can be changed as Black men become more actively involved in their personal development and support other Black men in reaching their full potential.

For far too long, Black men have operated in isolation from one another rather than relying on one another for support. Breaking away from the mainstream stereotypes of Black men and the preconceived notions of what it means to be a Black man will take a concerted effort that begins at the community level. One such initiative, Black Men Build, is based on community men's circles where Black men can be themselves, engage in conversation, and receive education about overcoming their struggles. The program also offers political and civic education to organize Black men around engagement in various economic, political, and health issues. This type of model at the community level will engage Black men in an initiative that supports them, their families and their communities.

The question of how this can be implemented in every local community level must be answered. This is where the Black church comes in. As the center of every Black community, the Black church has a crucial role in this initiative. Black churches have the power to lead the way in building a community of strong and engaged Black men by collaborating with local organizations to identify a location for such meetings and spreading the word throughout the community. Whether the Black church is in an urban or rural community, it is the powerhouse of the Black community. Therefore, engaging Black churches in a community initiative to build mentorships and partnerships that support Black men will be critical.

Black men in positions of business and economic leadership must also be engaged in the initiative because they can highlight how resilient social networks and partnerships can help Black men overcome the problems they face. Although the initiative will be powered at the grassroots level, creating national awareness of the initiative will be essential.

Building Professional Networks for Black Men

In addition to building community networks for mentorship, there is a need to create a broad professional support network for and among Black men. Professional networks will allow Black men to make professional connections that help them progress in their occupations and overcome the existing racism they face as they build solid professional identities (Wingfield, 2014; Hawkins, 2022; Palmer, 2008; Strayhorn & Johnson, 2020). This is particularly important for Black men who did not attend elite schools and lack the social and professional connections needed to succeed since professional networks support success (Spriggs et al., 2020). Just as in other areas, Black men need professional mentoring to advance successfully (Hawkins, 2022; Palmer et al., 2008).

Although professional organizations do exist for Black men, such as the African American Chamber of

Commerce and the African American Strategy Group (AASC), more professional networks must be constructed to assist Black men by providing the support and mentoring they need to realize success in the professional setting (Harley et al., 2020; Hawkins, 2022). It is possible to form such groups at the local level to assist Black men in connecting with and supporting one another in the professional setting, particularly as older, more successful Black men mentor younger Black men.

Involving Black Men in Self-Advocacy and Activism

The information reviewed in this book demonstrates how involvement in advocacy and activism results in a higher level of well-being for Black men (Alexander et al., 2023; Hotchkins, 2017; Roberts, 2023; Turner et al., 2022). By developing professional and community networks and partnering with churches and community organizations, Black men can build a solid network of collaboration for self-advocacy that will assist them collectively in creating a better future for themselves, their families, and their communities.

Building social networks within the community will assist Black men in connecting with one another so they can mentor and be mentored in various areas of their lives, including their relationships, spirituality, and professional lives. These connections will also help them form a vibrant community of like-minded Black men who work together to create a better future for Black boys and men.

Self-advocacy network-building will support Black men as they work together to address all the areas of their lives where they experience systemic racism and discrimination, fight against stereotypes, and develop a positive identity in all areas.

Going National with an Awareness Initiative

Creating a national awareness initiative on Black men's empowerment will require the larger and more prominent Black churches to coordinate with the larger Historically Black Colleges and Universities (HBCUs) to build a program model for grassroots initiatives. Ideally, the model would include mental health and wellness education, family and relationships, economic and social empowerment, and networking and alliances to help Black men. A mentorship model should be developed to assist grassroots efforts by matching older and younger Black men in mentoring relationships.

It is crucial that the initiative be church-led to ensure that Black men have the opportunity for spiritual development and growth in tandem with development in the other essential areas of their lives. Spirituality is central to the African-American culture, and the failure to include that aspect in any program focused on helping Black men develop more resilience would mean essentially leaving out the most necessary ingredient for healthy development.

However, the national initiative should not develop a program that is rigidly set out. Instead, it should offer the basic framework of the areas that should be included in the program, allowing localities to adapt the framework to the specific needs of the Black male population in their community. The national initiative will provide the impetus needed to build awareness of community programs and facilitate the announcement and spread of information so that Black men throughout the United States are aware that local initiatives are being implemented to help them navigate the difficulties they face in various areas of their lives.

It would be helpful to have well-known Black men involved in the campaign to draw more attention to the initiative. Little funding will be required because local community initiatives can meet in churches or other central locations in the community. The initiative will be led by volunteers willing to devote their time and energy to building stronger and more resilient Black men, knowing that the wider community will realize enormous benefits when Black men are empowered to positively impact their communities and society.

The National Black Church Initiative would be an ideal organization to lead the national information awareness initiative because it is a coalition of more than 150,000 African-American churches in the United States with more than 27 million members. It is already focused on eliminating racial disparities in various areas, such as education, housing, and healthcare. The National Black Church initiative also has a website that could help disseminate information about the initiative to the broader national community of African Americans and their churches.

Changing the Mindset

The first step in changing the perspectives of Black men and promoting their healing is changing their mindset. The information presented in this book is essential to understanding the myriad problems Black men face in their lives and communities. There is a saying that "Rome was not built in a day," and the same is true for addressing the struggles of Black men due to the generational problems that have plagued them since the days of slavery.

Although slavery has been illegal in the United States for a century and a half, the issues arising from slavery persist. The most formidable barrier to the success of Black men in every area of their lives is their mindset. That mindset has been driven by racism, discrimination, unfair criminal justice system practices, and challenges in building strong communities of Black men that stand together, support one another, and provide the strength to rise above the challenges.

Black men must develop strong and positive self-identity and envision themselves as successful in all areas of their lives. However, for far too many Black men, their developmental years were marked by poverty, broken homes, failing schools, and high-crime neighborhoods.

The support that Black men need must begin early in their lives and continue as they enter school. This requires Black men in the community to mentor Black boys from an early age and provide ongoing support throughout their school, university, and adult years.

Although the Black church has offered some support in this area, too many young Black males are no longer attending church, which has removed much of the positive influence from their lives. It will take a concerted community effort over many years to build the capacity of Black men to mentor younger Black men.

Many initiatives already exist but need to be expanded. From mentoring young Black males in schools, to mentoring adult Black males post-incarceration, to mentoring Black men in the workplace, Black men need role models and social networks to develop the strength and capacity to overcome their challenges.

The strategies outlined in this book provide a foundation for this effort, but further development is required. It is beyond the scope of this book to determine what is needed in each community to address the societal ills and challenges that Black men face. However, it is clear from the research in this book that building social networks for Black men in every aspect of their lives is critical to supporting their resilience and success.

Mentoring, teaching, and guidance in the lives of Black men are vital.

A Question of Policy

There are actions that policymakers can take to address the challenges and barriers faced by Black men. Although some changes in laws have addressed the incredible over-incarceration of Black men, more can be done, as research shows that Black men are incarcerated at higher rates than White men. Often, Black men do not have the resources needed to pay for effective legal representation. Strengthening legal representation for Black men will require changes in policies and funding to ensure that every Black man who is arrested has sufficient legal representation. Moves have been made in some locations in the United States to address the problems associated with the inability of those living in poverty to pay bail so they can be released before trial, but those initiatives should go further.

Another problem that has been cited is the lack of Black male teachers and mental health providers. Improving grant funding so Black males can gain access to universities and earn a degree in those areas is needed.

Finally, policymakers should allocate more funding to underserved, primarily Black communities in urban and rural areas. An intense focus should exist on creating a better community environment for Black children to grow and thrive. Far too often, Black communities are on the receiving end of the scraps of funding allocations, which results in those living in the communities feeling unvalued. Additionally, this book has revealed that policymakers are not addressing the social determinants of health for Black communities, particularly their living environments.

Therefore, policymakers should examine communities that have landfills, chemical exposure, and other unhealthy industries relegated to predominantly Black communities and ensure that they do not suffer from severe environmental contamination, which negatively affects their physical health outcomes. However, gaining the notice and consensus of policymakers to move toward those changes will require coordination and collaboration among Black men, as has been recommended in community initiatives to drive change at the personal, interpersonal, intrapersonal, and broader societal levels.

Black men must organize to build one another up and, in doing so, work cooperatively to mount pressure for needed policy changes. As Black men are empowered locally and in their own lives, they will become more empowered to work collectively toward driving changes in their communities.

Conclusion

Black men are resilient in the face of systemic racism, discrimination, stereotypes, and stigma. Despite the problems experienced due to race and gender, many Black men have overcome their challenges and serve as shining beacons of hope to other Black men.

African American culture is rooted in community and extended family, so the value of support is deeply ingrained in Black men and their lives. However, in contemporary society, the struggles faced by Black men are often in the context of a broken family during their earlier years, which means they do not have a father figure or positive role model. As a result, they need more connections in their lives to provide the necessary support for healthy development and life success.

The challenges faced by Black men can be overcome by building connections with mentors and through social networks where they can find support and role models. Developing caring relationships that nurture their personal growth and success in all areas of life is also essential. Yet, for many Black men, those resources are lacking, especially for Black men in dire socioeconomic circumstances, those who have experienced incarceration, or those who may have mental or physical health disabilities.

Black men struggle to overcome their conception of what constitutes Black male masculinity, which leaves them believing they cannot admit to needing help or support. However, the guidance they receive from sources they do not trust is often inadequate. Therefore, there is a need to build a coalition of support for Black males from sources they trust.

As the Black church, Black male professionals, and leaders work collaboratively with organizations to create a support system that Black males can access, they will be more likely to become engaged and seek the help they need to succeed. Whether Black men need therapy, mentoring for personal and professional development, or just a social network where they can feel accepted and belong, healing can only come when Black men reach out to one another and guide each other toward a better way of living.

I hope this book has offered information that will help Black men gain a deeper understanding of the necessity of reaching out to one another and building supportive relationships that assist them with healing in all areas of their lives.

References

African American Chamber of Commerce and African American Strategy Group (AASC) (2024). https://theaachamber.com/

Alexander, A. C., Waring, J. J. C., Noble, B., Bradley, D., Olurotimi, O., Fronheiser, J., Sifat, M., Ehlke, S. J., Boozary, L. K., McQuoid, J., & Kendzor, D. E. (2023). Perceptions of mental health and exploring the role of activism among African Americans exposed to media coverage of police brutality and protests. *Journal of Racial and Ethnic Health Disparities, 10,* 1403-1413. https://doi.org/10.1007/s40615-022-01326-2

Archibald, P. (2019). Perspective: Work-related stress and mortality among Black men. *Ethnicity and Disease, 29*(1), 21-22. Doi: 10.18865/ed.29.1.21

Auxier, B. (2020). *Social media continues to be important political outlets for Black Americans.* Pew Research Center, 11 December. https://www.pewresearch.org/short-reads/2020/12/11/social-media-continue-to-be-important-political-outlets-for-black-americans/

Avent, J. R., & Cashwell, C. S. (2015). The Black church: Theology and implications for counseling African Americans. *The Professional Counselor, 5*(1), 81-90. Doi: 10.15241/jra.5.1.81

Aweah, E. A. (2023). *I say who I am: Black males and building our identity,* 30 March. https://www.childrensdefense.org/blog/i-say-who-i-am-black-males-and-building-our-identity/

Bae, D., & Kogan, S. M. (2020). Romantic relationships trajectories among young African American men: The influence of adverse life contexts. *Journal of Family Psychology, 34*(6), 687-697. Doi: 10.1037/fam0000645.

Bannon, W. M., McKay, M. M., Chacko, A., Rodriguez, J. A., & Cavaleri, M. (2009). Cultural pride reinforcement as a dimension of racial socialization protective of urban African American child anxiety. *Families in Society, 90*(1), 79-86. Doi: 10.1606/1044-3894.3848

Barber, K. H. (2014). Wither shall we go? The past and present of Black churches and the public sphere. *Religions, 20*(6), 245-265. Doi: 10.3390/rel6010245

Barton, A. W., Beach, S. R. H., Wells, A. C., Ingels, J. B., Corso, P. S., Sperr, M. C., Anderson, T. N., & Brody, G. H. (2018). The Protecting Strong African American Families Program: A randomized controlled trial with rural African American couples. *Prevention Science, 19*(7), 904-913. Doi: 10.1007/s11121-018-0895-4.

Being Black in corporate America: An intersectional exploration. Center for Talent and Innovation, 1-13. https://coqual.org/wp-content/uploads/2020/09/CoqualBeing BlackinCorporateAmerica090720-1.pdf

Bell, R. A. (2019). A point of view: *Redefining the Black male role model in education and mentorship*. The Inclusion Solution. https://theinclusionsolution.me/a-point-of-view-redefining-the-black-male-role-model-in-education-and-mentorship/

Benjamin S. Carson, M.D. (2024). Achievement.org. https://achievement.org/achiever/benjamin-s-carson/

Beverley, M., Holson, D. A., & Hewlett, D. (2022). Patient engagement and cultural sensitivity as a strategy to improve health inequities: The solutions are as simple as they are complex. *Journal of the National Medical Association,* 4(6), 578-583. Doi: 10.1016/j.jnma.2022.09.005

Bieber, J. P. (2023). *The effects of musical frequency and interval on meditation.* Conference: 2023 Sofia University Global Conference on Advancing Mental Health: At Sofia University, 1-14. https://www.researchgate.net/publication/381662938_The_Effects_of_Musi cal_Frequency_and_Interval_on_Meditation

About (2024) Black Men Build. https://www.blackmen.build/about/

Boots on the Ground, Putting Community First (2024). Black Men United.

https://blackmenunitedusa.org/

Briscoe, D. L. (2017). *Distinctive feature of the African-American family: Debunking the myth of the deficit model.* [University of Arkansas: Little Rock, Arkansas], 1-26. https://scholarscompass.vcu.edu/cgi/viewcontent.cgi?article=1132&context=esr

Brown, A. K. (2013). Cultural perspective on African American culture. *International Journal of Education &*

Literacy Studies, 1(2), 54-68. Doi: :10.7575/aiac.ijels.v.1n.2p.54

Brown, A. K. (2013). Cultural perspective on African American culture. *International Journal of Education & Literacy Studies, 1*(2), 54-68.

Brown, G. L., Kogan, S. M., & Kim, J. (2019). From fathers to sons: The intergenerational transmission of parenting behavior among African American young men. *Family Processes, 57*(1), 165-180. Doi: 10.1111/famp.12273

Buckley, T. R. (2018). Black adolescent males: Intersections among their gender role identity and racial identity and associations with self-concept (global and school). *Child Development, 89*(4), 1-18. Doi: 10.1111/cdev.12950.

Building on the legacy of the 100 (2019). 100 Black Men of America, Inc, 1-33.

https://100blackmen.org/wp-content/uploads/2020/07/2019-Annual-Report_opt.pdf

Burrowes, A. M. (2019). *Post traumatic slave syndrome: A literature review on African American Community Healing and Expressive Arts Therapy*. [Capstone Theses, 200] [Cambridge, MA: Lesley University], 1-40.

https://digitalcommons.lesley.edu/cgi/viewcontent.cgi?article=1191&context=expressive_theses

Chakraverty, D., (2020). The imposter syndrome among Black doctoral and postdoctoral scholars in STEM. *International Journal of Doctoral Studies (IJDS)*, *15*, 433-460. https://doi.org/10.28945/4613

Chaney, C., & Mincey, K. D. (2014). Typologies of Black male sensitivity in R&B and Hip Hop. *Journal of Hip Hop Studies*, *1*(1)(9), 1-36. https://scholarscompass.vcu.edu/cgi/viewcontent.cgi?article=1008&context=jhhs

Chime in the community: Our partnership with 100 Black men (2021). Medium. https://medium.com/life-at-chime/chime-in-the-community-our-partnership-with-100-black-men-dbd32c008da1

Chung, B., Meldrum, M., Jones, F., Brown, A., Daaood, R., & Jones, L. (2014). Perceived sources of stress and resilience in men in an African-American community. *Progress in Community Health Partnerships, 8*(4), 441-451. Doi: 10.1353/cpr.2014.0053.

Cokley, K. O., Bernard, D. L., Stone-Sabali, S., & Awad, G. H. (2024). Imposter syndrome in racially/ethically minoritized groups: Current Knowledge and Future Directions. *Annual Review of Clinical Psychology, 20*, 407-430. https://doi.org/10.1146/annurev-clinpsy-081122-015724

Collins, D. J. (2022). Mentoring urban African American students in secondary school. *College of Education Theses and Dissertations, 245*, 1-76. https://via.library.depaul.edu/cgi/viewcontent.cgi?article=1234&context=soe_etd

Combest, A. J. (2022). *Black males and the Baptist church: A phenomenological study of participation and attendance in Columbus, Ohio.* [Doctoral Dissertations] [Ashland University: Ashland, OH], 1-119.

https://etd.ohiolink.edu/acprod/odb_etd/ws/send_file/send?accession=ashland1667229890229689&disposition=inline

Connell, C. L., Wang, S. C., Crook, L., & Yadrick, K. (2019). Barriers to healthcare seeking and provision among African American adults in the rural Mississippi Delta region: Community and provider perspectives. *Journal of Community Health, 44*(4), 636-645. Doi: 10.1007/s10900-019-00620-1.

Cooper, S. M., Robbins, P. A., Burnett, M., & McBride, N. (2020). African American fathers' coping patterns: Implications for father-son involvement and race-related discussions. *Journal of Applied Development Psychology, 70*, 1-21. https://doi.org/10.1016/j.appdev.2020.101163

Cooper, W. C. (2024). Growing healthy churches in the Black community through the introduction and implementation of spiritual formation and soul care. *ProQuest, 31244218*.

Copeland, K. (2022). *African American artists find release and healing through creativity*, 16 August. https://www.ideastream.org/news/community/2022-08-16/african-american-artists-find-release-and-healing-through-creativity

Cozart, H. (2016). *The impact of spiritual mentoring among African American males at Eastern Kentucky University*. [Asbury Theological Seminary: Wilmore, Kentucky], 1-108. https://place.asburyseminary.edu/cgi/viewcontent.cgi?article=1 845&context=ecommonsatsdissertations

Crook, T., Thomas, C. M., & Cobia, D. C. (2009). Masculinity and sexuality: Impact on intimate relationships of African American men. *The Family Journal: Counseling and Therapy for Couples and Families, 17*(4), 360-366. Doi: 10.1177/1066480709347304

Cross, C. J., Taylor, R. J., & Chatters, L. M. (2018). Family social support networks of African American and Black Caribbean adolescents. *Journal of Family Studies, 27*(9), 2727-2771. Doi: 10.1007/s10826-018-1116-2

Cummings, T. E. (2019). African American male entrepreneurs: A study of the key success factors. *Education Doctoral, 423,* 1-151. https://fisherpub.sjf.edu/cgi/viewcontent.cgi?article=1429&context=education_etd

Daymond John on focus, fashion, and finding the right mentor (2020). The Wharton School. https://www.wharton.upenn.edu/story/daymond-john-on-focus-fashion-and-finding-the-right-mentor/

Dear Mama. 2Pac Track 22. (N. D.). Genius.com. https://genius.com/2pac-dear-mama-lyrics

Du Bois, W. E. B. (2023). The souls of Black folks. E-Book. Amazon Publishers, 1-165.

Eley, N. T., Namey, E., Mckenna, K., Johnson, A. C., & Guest, G. (2019). Beyond the individual: Social and cultural influences on the health-seeking behaviors of African American men. *American Journal of Men's Health, 13*(1), 1-11. Doi: 10.1177/1557988319829953

English, B. L. (2016). Spirituality, religion, and pursuing purpose: Connecting African American males' educational pursuits to a higher power. *The Journal of Faith, Education, and Community, 1*(3), 1-43. https://scholarworks.sfasu.edu/jfec/vol1/iss1/3

Farmer, G. L. (2006). African American males' civic engagement: The importance of social organization involvement and friendship diversity. *Journal of African American Studies, 10*(2), 52-68. Doi: 10.1007/s12111-006-1003-6

Gaydos, S. (2021). *Byron Allen's entertainment education came from the giants at NBC.* https://variety.com/2021/tv/features/byron-allen-entertainment-education-nbc-1235090709/

Ghose, S. K. (2019). The role of the Black church in the American Civil Rights Movement. *Journal of University of Information Technology & Sciences (UITS),*

5(1), 58-68. https://uits.edu.bd/wp-content/uploads/2019/06/05-The-Role-of-the-Black-Church-in-the-58-68.pdf

Gilbert, K. L., Ray, R., Siddiai, A., Shetty, S., Baker, E. A., Elder, K., & Griffith, D. M. (2016). Visible and invisible trends in Black men's health: Pitfalls and promises for addressing racial, ethnic, and gender inequities in health. *Annual Review of Public Health, 37*, 295-311. Doi: 10.1146/annurev-publhealth-032315-021556.

Gilchrist, G. (2006). *Loneliness, Black men, and friendships: Part I.*

https://thesuperspade.wordpress.com/2006/07/27/loneliness-black-men-and-friendships-3/

Givens, J. R., Nasir, N., Roll, K., & D. Royston, M. M. (2016). Modeling manhood: Reimaging Black male identities. *Anthropology and Education Quarterly, 47*(2), 167-185. Doi: 10.1111/aeq.12147

Goldsby, T. L., Goldsby, M. E., McWalters, M., & Mills, P. J. (2022). Sound healing: Mood, emotional, and spiritual well-being interrelationships. *Religions, 13*(123), 1-12. https://doi.org/10.3390/rel13020123

Grawert, A., & Cragie, T. A. (2020). *Mass incarceration has been a driving force of economic inequality*. Brennan Center for Justice. https://www.brennancenter.org/our-work/analysis-opinion/mass-incarceration-has-been-driving-force-economic-inequality

Green, M. (2024). From spirituals to today: Black artists historically use music to promote freedom. *The Washington Informer*, 7 February.

https://wordinblack.com/2024/02/from-spirituals-to-today-black-artists-historically-use-music-to-promote-freedom/

Greenlee, D. (2013). Living out an 'in Christ' identity: Research and reflections related to Muslims who have come to faith in Jesus Christ. *International Journal of Frontier Missiology, 30*(1), 1-8.

https://www.ijfm.org/PDFs_IJFM/30_1_PDFs/IJFM_30_1-Greenlee.pdf

Green-Powell, P. (2012). The rewards of mentoring. *US-China Education Review, B*(1), 99-106. ISSN 1548-6613. https://files.eric.ed.gov/fulltext/ED531660.pdf

Griffith, D. M., & Semlow, A. R. (2020). Art, anti-racism and health equity: "Don't ask me why, ask me how!" *Ethnicity & Disease, 30*(3), 373-380.

https://pmc.ncbi.nlm.nih.gov/arti cles/PMC7360189/pdf/ethndis-30-373.pdf

Grimes, E. K. (2014). Guide to recruitment Black men as mentors for Black Boys. Journal of Community Psychology, 28 (4), 391 – 406. *Journal of Community Psychology, 28* (4), 391 – 406.

Gwathmey, T. M., Williams, K. L., Caban-Holt, A., Starks, T. D., Foy, C. G., Mathews, A., & Byrd, G. S. (2024). Building a community partnership for the development of health ministries within the African American Community: The Triad Pastors Network. *Journal of Community Health, 49*, 559-567. https://doi.org/10.1007/s10900-023-01315

Halloran, M. J. (2018). African American health and posttraumatic slave syndrome: A terror management theory. *Journal of Black Studies, 50*(1).

https://journals.sagepub.com/doi/10.1177/0021934718803737

Harley, A. E., Frazer, D., Weber, T., Edwards, T. C., & Carnegie, N. (2020). No longer an island: A social network intervention engaging Black men through CBPR. *American Journal of Men's Health*, 1-13. Doi: 10.1177/1557988320913387

Harris, J., & Kruger, A. C. (2022). "Be kind but not too kind": Black Males' prosocial behaviors in the face of dehumanization. *Journal of Research on Adolescence, 32*(2), 552-569. Doi: 10.1111/jora.12746

Harris, J., & Kruger, A. C. (2022). 'Be Kind but not too kind': Black males' prosocial behaviors in the face of dehumanization. *Journal of Research on Adolescence, 32*(2), 552-568. Doi: 10.1111/jora.12746

Harris, S. M. (1995). Psychosocial development and Black male masculinity: Implications for counseling economically disadvantaged African American male adolescents. *Journal of Counseling and Development (JCD), 73*, 279-286.

Hawkins, A. J. (2022). Professional Black men and their developmental relationships with career mentors and sponsors. [Minneapolis, MN: ScholarWorks, Walden University], 1-170. https://scholarworks.waldenu.edu/cgi/viewcontent.cgi?article=14683&context=dissertations

Holden, K. B., McGregor, B. S., Blanks, S. H., & Pharmd, C. M. (2012). Psychosocial, socio-cultural, and environmental influences on mental health help-seeking among African American men. *Journal of Men's Health, 9*(2), 63-69. https://doi.org/10.1 016/j.jomh.2012.03.002

Hosikison, M. (2022). *Byron Allen: What to know about the media mogul, from comedian to possible NFL team owner.* Montgomery Advertiser, 4 March. https://www.montgomeryadvertiser.com/story/news/2022/03/04/byron-allen-6-things-know-mogul-behind-allen-media-group/9362832002/

Hotchkins, B. K. (2017). Black student leaders practicing resistance in the midst of chaos: Applying transgenerational activist knowledge to navigate a predominantly White institution. *The Journal of Negro Education, 86*(3), 269-282.

http://www.jstor.org/stable/10.7709/jnegroeducation.86.3.0269

Howard, T. C., Flennaugh, T. K., & Terry, C. L. (2012). Black males, social imagery, and the disruption of pathological identities: Implications for research and teaching. *Educational Foundations (Winter-Spring)*, 1-18. https://files.eric.ed.gov/fulltext/EJ968819.pdf

Hurt, T. R. (2013). Toward a deeper understanding of the meaning of marriage among Black men. *Journal of Family Issues, 34*(7), 859-994. Doi: 10.1177/0192513X12451737

Hurt, T. R. (2014). Black men and the decision to marry. *Marriage and Family Review, 50*(6), 447-479. Doi: 10.1080/01494929.2014.905816.

Hwang, W., Kim, J. H., Brown, M. T., & Silverstein, M. (2023). Intergenerational solidarity of adult children with parents emerging to established adulthood. Journal of Family Psychology, 37(6), 853-963. Doi: 10.1037/fam0001087

Hyman, J. B. (2006). *Men and communities: African American males and the well-being of children, families, and neighborhoods.* The Joint Center Health Policy Institute,

1-33. https://www.nationalcollaborative.org/wp-content/uploads/2016/02/Men-and-Communities.pdf

Jack, L., & Griffith, D. M. (2016). The health of African American men: Implications for research and practice. *American Journal of Men's Health, 7*(4), 1-4. Doi: 10.1177/1557988313490190.

Jackson, C. (2020) *"In my feelings": Millennial African Americans' perceptions, understanding, and experience of health romantic relationships* [Master's thesis, Minnesota State University, Mankato]. Cornerstone: A Collection of Scholarly and Creative Works for Minnesota State University, Mankato. https://cornerstone.lib.mnsu.edu/etds/1059/

Jacob, G., Faber, S. C., Faber, N., Bartlett, A., Ouimet, A. J., & Williams, M. T. (2023). A systematic review of Black people coping with racism: Approaches, analysis, and empowerment. *Perspectives on Psychological Science, 18*(2), 392-415. Doi: 10.1177/17469162211100509.

Jenkins, T. S. (2011). A beautiful mind: Black male intellectual identity and hip-hop culture. *Journal of Black Studies*, 1-12. Doi: 10.1177/0021934711405050

John, D. (2024). Mentors who changed my life. https://daymondjohn.com/blogs/jou rnal/84017732-mentors-who-changed-my-life

Johnson, A. M., & Godsil, R. D. (N. D.). *Transforming perception: Black men and boys: Executive Summary*. Black Male Reimagined II.

https://equity.ucla.edu/wp-content/uploads/2016/11/Transforming-Perception.pdf

Johnson, V. E., & Carter, R. T. (2020). Black cultural strengths and psychological well-being an empirical analysis with Black American Adults. *Journal of Black Psychology, 46*(1), 55-89. Doi: 10.1177/0095798419889752

Jones, A. L., Rafferty, J., Cochran, S. D., Abelson, J., Hanna, M. R., & Mays, V. M. (2022). Prevalence, severity, and burden of post-traumatic stress disorder in Black men and women across the adult lifespan. Journal of Aging Health, 34(3), 401-412. Doi: 10.1177/08982643221086071

Jones, K. (2011). *Analyzing the social political activism of the Black church in light of the two-kingdoms motif.* https://www.modernreformation.org/resources/articles/analyzing-the-social-political-activism-of-the-black-church-in-light-of-the-two-kingdoms-motif

Jones-Eversley, S. D., Rice, J., Adedoyin, A. C., & James-Townes, L. (2020). Premature deaths of young Black males in the United States. *Journal of Black Studies, 3.* https://doi.org/10.1177/0021934719895999

Jordan, H., Jeremiah, R., & Watson, K. (2024). Exploring preventive health care utilization among Black/African American men. *American Journal of Men's Health*, 1-12. Doi: 10.1177/15579883231225548

Joseph, J. J., Nolan, T. S., Brock, G., Williams, A., Zhao, S., McKoy, A., Kluwe, B., Metlock, F. Campanelli, K., Odei, J. B., Khumalo, M. T., Lavender, D., Gregory, J., & Gray, D. M. (2024). Improving mental health in Black men through a 24-week community-based lifestyle change intervention: The Black impact program. BMC Psychiatry, 24(34), 1-14. https://bmcpsychiatry.biomedcentral.com/articles/10.1186/s12888-023-05064-5

Joseph, J. J., Nolan, T. S., Brock, G., Williams, A., Zhao, S., McKoy, A., Kluwe, B., Metlock, F., Campanelli, K., Odei, J. B., Khumalo, M. T., Lavender, D., Gregory, J., & Gray, D. M. (2024). Improving mental health in Black men through a 24-week community-based lifestyle change intervention: The Black impact program. *BMC Psychiatry, 24*(34), 1-14. https://doi.org/10.1186/s12888-023-05064-5

Julion, W. A., Breitenstein, S. M., & Waddell, D. (2012). Fatherhood intervention in collaboration with African American non-resident fathers. *Research in Nursing and Health, 35*(5), 490-506. Doi: 10.1002/nur.21492

Kogan, S. M., Yu, T., & Brown, G. L. (2016). Romantic relationship commitment behavior among emerging African American Men. *Journal of Marriage and Family, 78*(4), 996-1012. Doi: 10.1111/jomf.12293

Kogan, S. M., Yu, T., & Brown, G. L. (2016). Romantic relationships commitment behavior among emerging adult African American men. *Journal of Marriage and Family, 78*(4), 996-1012. Doi: 10.1111/jomf.12293.

Lewis, D., & Hong, P. Y. (2020). Incapacitated fatherhood: The impact of mass incarceration on Black father identity, Qualitative Criminology, 8(3). https://www.qualitati vecriminology.com/pub/v8i3p4/release/4

Lincoln, C. E., & Mamiya, L. H. (2003). *The Black church in the African American experience.* 13th ed. [Durham and London: Duke University Press], 1-808.

Lindsey, M. A., & Marcell, A. V. (2012). We're going through a lot of struggles that people don't even know about': The need to understand African American males' help-seeking for mental health on multiple levels. *American Journal of Men's Health, 6*(5), 354-364. Doi: 10.1177/1557988312441520

Logan, J. R. (2013). The persistence of segregation in the 21st century metropolis. *City Community, 12*(2), 1-10. Doi: :10.1111/cico.12021

Martin, T., (2022). Embodying the Black/African American experience through collaborative improvised music and dance/movement: Implications for the practice of music therapy. *Qualitative Inquiries in Music Therapy, 16*(3), 71-102. https://barcelonapublishers.com/resources/QIMT16/03_Martin.pdf

Mattis, J., & Grayman-Simpson, N. (2013). Faith and the sacred in African American life. Chapter 30. In *APA Handbook of Psychology, Religion, & Spirituality, 1.*

Kenneth Pargament (ed.), 547-564. Doi: 10.1037/14045-030

McCluney, L., Bryant, C. M., King, D. D., & Ali, A. A. (2017). Calling in Black: A dynamic model of racially traumatic events, resourcing, and safety. *International Journal of Equality, Diversity, and Inclusion, 36*(8), 767-786. https://doi.org/10.1108/EDI-01-2017-0012

Melson-Silimon, A., Spivey, B. N., & Skinner-Dorkenoo, A. L. (2023). The construction of racial stereotypes and how they serve racial propaganda. *Social and Personality Psychology Compass*, 1-20. Doi: 10.1111/spc3.12862

Mitchell, K. (2021). *The resilience of Black love in history.* Black Perspectives, 12 February. https://www.aaihs.org/the-resilience-of-black-love-in-black-history/

Mizelle, D. L. (2023). "Meet me at the altar" heterosexual Black men and marriage: A content analysis. *Spectrum Journal on Black Men, 10*(2), 99-112. https://doi.org/10.2 979/spe.2023.a903153

N'Guessan, K. E. (2022). The absence-presence configuration of Black being: Signifying enslavement and resistance in Colson Whitehead's the Underground Railroad. *International Journal on Studies in English Language and Literature (IJSELL), 10*(9), 6-16. https://doi.org/10.20431/2347-3134.1009002

Napierala, P. (2021). Black churches and African American social activism: The 'opiate view' and the 'inspiration view' of Black religion in the selected literature. *B.A.S., XXVII*, 95-111.

National Black Church Initiative (2024). https://www.naltblackchurch.com/index.php

Nguyen, A. W., Chatters, L. M., Taylor, R. J., & Mouzon, D. M. (2016). Social support from family and friends and subjective well-being of older African Americans. *Journal of Happiness Studies, 17*(3), 959-979. Doi: 10.1007/s10902-015-9626-8.

Nguyen, A. W., Taylor, R. J., Chatters, L. M., & Hope, M. O. (2020). Church support networks of African Americans: The impact of gender and religious involvement. *Journal of Community Psychology, 47*(5), 1043-1063. Doi: 10.1002/jcop.22171

Ngyuen, A. W., Chatters, L. M., & Taylor, R. J. (2016). African American extended family and church-based social network typologies. *Interdisciplinary Journal of Applied Family Studies, 65*, 701-715. Doi: 10.1111/fare.12218

Okoro, O. N., Nelson, C. S., Witherspoon, S. P. Witherspoon. S. F., & Simmons, G. E. (2020). Culturally responsive health promotion to address health disparities in African American men: A program impact evaluation. *American Journal of Men's Health*, 1-14. https://doi.org/10.1177/1557988320951321

Owens, M. A., McKnight, J., Tiner, M., & Dunlap, R. R. (2020). The Black church and liberal arts institutions: Forming reciprocal relationships for thriving urban communities and churches. *Metropolitan Universities, 31*(3), 181-196. Doi: 10.18060/24058

Palmer, G. A., & Johnson-Bailey, J. (2008). The impact of mentoring on the careers of African Americans. *Canadian Journal of Career Development*, 7(1), 45-51. https://cjcd-rcdc.ceric.ca/index.php/cjcd/article/download/263/251

Pantin, L. E. (2021). Race and equity in the age of unicorns. *72 Hastings Law Journal, 1453*, 1-59.

https://scholarship.law.columbia.edu/cgi/viewcontent.cgi?article=399 8&context=faculty_scholarship

Park, C. L., Holt, C. L., Le, D., Christie, J., & Williams, B. R (2017). Positive and negative religious coping styles as prospective predictors of well-being in African American. *American Psychological Association*, 1-28. https://dx.doi.org/10.1037/rel0000124

Pathak, E. B. (2017). Mortality among Black men in the United States, *Journal of Racial and Ethnic Health Disparities, 5*(1), 50-61. Doi: 10.1007/s40615-017-0341-5.

Pederson, A. B., Hawkins, D., & Conteh, N. (2022). Ethnic identity and mental health stigma among Black adults in the United States. *Ethics, Medicine, and Public Health, 25*, 1-22. https://doi.org/10.1016/j.jemep.2022.100774

Phillips, J. M., Branch, C. J., Brady, S. S., & Simpson, T. (2018). Parents speak: A needs assessment for community programming for Black male youth. *American Journal of Preventive Medicine, 55*, 81-82. https://doi.org/10.1016/j.amepre.2018.05.014

Pough, S. L. (2019). *Transgenerational trauma: The effects of slavery on African American male leadership.*

[Sarasota, FL: Argosy University], 1-209. https://media.proquest.com /media/hms/PFT/2/BjBcI? s=%2BSQi4R0X1bW90Mux kA1WfpYBbvQ%3D

Priest, J. B., Smith, S. M., Woods, S. B., & Roberson, P. N. E. (2020). Discrimination, family emotional climate, and African American health: An application of the BBFM. Journal of Family Psychology, 34(5), 598-609. http://dx.doi.org/10.1037/fam0000621

Racial and ethnic disparities in PTSD (2020). National Center for PTSD. *PTSD Research Quarterly, 31*(4), 1-12. https://www.ptsd.va.gov/publications/rq_docs/V31N4.pdf

Reed, D. D., & Adams, R. (2020). A social-ecological perspective of spiritual resilience and suicidality among African-American men. *Social Work in Public Health*, 1-13. Doi: 10.1080/19371918.2020.1824845

Tate, G. J. (2023). The decline of Black men's church attendance: The role of male presence in church and the family. [Doctoral of Ministry] [George Fox University,

Newburg: OR], 1-136. https://digitalcommons.georgefox.edu/dmin/560

Rice, T. M., Jenkins, A. I. C., McNeil Smith, S., Alexander, C., & McGregor, C. M. (2023). Racial discrimination and romantic relationship dynamics among Black Americans: A systematic review. *Journal of Family Theories and Review, 15,* 793-821. Doi: 10.1111/jftr.12535.

Ríos-González, O., Ramis-Salas, M., Peña-Axt, J. C., & Racionero-Plaza, S. (2021). Alternative friendships to improve men's health status. The impact of new alternative masculinities' approach. *International Journal of Environmental Research and Public Health, 18*(2188), 1-13. . https://doi.org/10.3390/ijerph18042188

Roberts, T. S. (2023). African Americans and activism: Exploring the impact on psychological well-being, *Journal for Social Action in Counseling & Psychology, 15*(1), 14-31. Doi: 10.33043/JSACP.15.1.14-31

Robinson, M. A., Jones-Eversley, S., Moore, S. E., Ravenell, J., & Adedoyin, A. C. (2018). Black male mental health and the Black Church: Advancing a collaborative partnership and research agenda. *Journal of Religion and*

Health, 57, 1095-1107. https://doi.or g/10.1007/s10943-018-0570-x

Rogers, T., & Mitchell, D. (2022). Hidden identity: A constructivist grounded theory of Black male identity development at Historically Black Colleges and Universities. *The Qualitative Report, 27*(1)(12), 2251-2257. https://doi.org/10.46743/2160-3715/2022.5718

Roque, L., Khattar, R., & Pathhak, A. (2022). *Black men and the U.S. economy: How the economic recovery is perpetuating systemic racism.* American Progress, 28 March. https://www.americanprogress.org/article/black-men-and-the-u-s-economy-how-the-economic-recovery-is-perpetuating-systemic-racism/

Ross, B. R. (2017). *We make a life by what we give: The impact of high school mentoring program on the perceptions and academic achievement of Black males.* Doctoral Dissertation, 1-119. https://scholarcommons.sc.edu/cgi/viewcontent.cgi?article=7789&context=etd

Ruggles, S. (1994). The origins of African-American family structure. *American Sociological Review*, 59, 135-

151. https://users.pop.umn.edu/~ruggl001/Articles/Af-Am-fam.pdf

Salinas, C, Elliott, K., Allen, K., McEwan, D., King, C., & Boldon, C. (2018). The role of spirituality for Black male community college students. *Community College Journal of Research and Practice*, 1-15. https://doi.org/10.1080/10668926.2018.1429961

Sánchez, B. (2016). *Mentoring for Black male youth*. National Mentoring Resource Center, 1-26. https://nationalmentoringresourcecenter.org/wp-content/uploads/2021/01/BlackM ales_Population_Review.pdf

Sandefur, T. (2020). Frederick Douglass and the American dream. *CATO Journal, Winter*. https://www.cato.org/cato-journal/winter-2020/frederick-douglass-american-dream

Schawalm, F. D., Zandavalli, R. B., De Castro Filho, E. D., & Lucchetti, G. (2021). Is there a relationship between spirituality/religiosity and resilience? A systematic review and meta-analysis of observational studies. *Journal of Health Psychology*, 1-15. Doi: https://doi.org/10.1177/1359105320984537

Scott-Jones, G., Kamara, M. R. (2020). The traumatic impact of structural racism on African Americans. *Delaware Journal of Public Health, 6*(5), 80-82. Doi: 10.32481/djph.202 0.11.019

Selvanathan, H. P., Jetten, J., & Umeh, A. (2021). A history of collective resilience and collective victimhood: Two sides of the same coin that explain Black Americans' present-day responses to oppression. *The British Psychological Society, 62*, 136-160. Doi: 10.1111/bjso.12562

Shikany, J. M., Schoenberger, Y. M., Konety, B. R., & Vickers, S. M. (2018). African American men's health: Research, Practice, and Policy. *American Journal of Preventive Medicine, 8*(55), 1-4. https://www.ajpmonline.org/action/showPdf?pii=S0749-3797%2818 %2932122-6

Smith, E. P., Yzaguirre, M. M., Dwanyen, L., & Wieling, E. (2022). Culturally relevant parenting approaches among African American and Latinx children and families: Toward resilient, strengths-based, trauma-informed practices. *Adversity and Resilience Science, 3*, 209-224. https://doi.org/10.1007/s42844-022-00059-9

Smith, M., Webstser, N., & Nayak, R. (2022). Exploring African American male youth's perceptions of community involvement through 4-H programs. *Journal of Youth Development, 17*(1), 10-31. Doi: 10.5195/jyd.2022.953

Smith, R. (2023). Black entrepreneurs: Breaking barriers and building dreams. https://robertsmith.com/blog/black-entrepreneurs/

Smith, R. F. (2023*). Black entrepreneurs: Breaking barriers and building dreams.* https://robertsmith.com/blog/black-entrepreneurs/

Spriggs, S. Jain-Link, P., & Kennedy, J. T. (2020). Black men in corporate America: Ambitious, driven, and blocked from the C-suite. *ELC Research Journal, Winter.* https://issuu.co m/elcinfo/docs/elc_institute_research_journal.winter_202 0.final/s/10260412

Strayhorn, T., & Johnson, R. M. (2014). Toward a framework for Black male professional identity. *NASAP Journal, 15*(2), 59-74. https://www.researchgate.net/publication/3400

Stuckey, H. L., & Nobel, J. (2010). The connection between art, healing, and public health: A review of current literature. *American Journal of Public Health, 100*, 254-263. Doi: 10.2105/AJPH

Tate, S. E. (2023). Is the Black church dead?: Religious resilience and the contemporary functions of Black Christianity. *Religions, 14*(460), 1=21. Doi: https://doi.org/ 10.3390/rel14040460

Taylor, J. (2024). *Dave Steward on building up the next generation of leaders*. https://helpingpeople.org/blog/dave-steward-world-wide-technologies-leadership-interview/

Taylor, R. J., Chatters, L. M., Nguyen, A. W., Taylor, H. O., Tsuchiya, K., & Ochoa, A. (2024). Friendship social networks of African Americans. *Sociological Focus*, 1-12. Doi: https://doi.org/10.1080/00380237.2024.2391042

Taylor, S. M. (2023). *4 organizations that are uplifting Black men.* https://www.ebony.com/4-organizations-that-are-uplifting-black-men/

Teti, M., Martin, A. E., Ranade, R., Massie, J., Malebranche, D. J., Tschann, J. M., & Bowleg, L. (2012).

"I'm a keep rising. I'm a keep going forward, regardless": Exploring Black men's resilience amid sociostructural challenges and stressors. *Qualitative Health Research, 22*(4), 524-533. Doi: 10.1177/1049732311422051

Thomas, E. (2024). Resilience in fatherhood: Exploring the impact of absent fathers on Black American men's parenting narratives and practices. *Electronic Theses, Projects, and Dissertations, 1876*, 1-81. https://scholarworks.lib.csusb.edu/cgi/viewcontent.cgi?articl e=3044&context=etd

Transforming perception: Black men and boys. Black Male Reimagined II. (N. D.). Perspective.org. https://equity.ucla.edu/wp-content/uploads/2016/11/Transforming-Perception.pdf

Turner, E. A., Douglas, C., & Haseeb, A. (2024). Predictors of seeking mental health treatment in Black men: Therapy fears and expectations about counseling. *Community Mental Health Journal, 60*, 385-393. https://doi.org/10.1007/s10597-023-01183-1

Turner, E. A., Harrell, S. P., & Bryant-Davis, T. (2022). Black love, activism, and community (BLAC): The BLAC model of healing and resilience. *Journal of Black*

Psychology, 48(3), 547-568. Doi: 10.1177/00957984211018364

Turner, E. A., Harrell, S. P., & Bryant-Davis, T. (2022). Black love, activism and community (BLAC): The BLAC model of healing and resilience. *Journal of Black Psychology, 48*(3), 547-568. Doi: https://doi.org/10.1177/00957984211018364

Turner, N. (2022). *5 Black heroes who took on the fight against mass incarceration.* Vera 22 February. https://www.vera.org/news/5-black-heroes-who-took-on-the-fight-against-mass-incarceration

Ugwuede, A. A. (2023). Post-traumatic stress disorder in African American men exposed to violent trauma. Archives of Psychiatric Nursing, 47, 44-46. https://doi.org/10.10 16/j.apnu.2023.10.005

Vecci, J. & Želinský, T. (2019). Behavioral challenges of minorities: Social identity and role models. *PLoS One, 14*(7)(e0220010), 1-21. Doi: 10.1371/journal.pone.0220010

Wang, M. (2023). Martin Luther King and the Civil Rights Movement in America. *Journal of Education, Humanities, and Social Sciences, 8*, 2262-2265. Doi: :10.54097/ehss.v8i.4686

Ward, E., Wiltshire, J. C., Detry, M. A., & Brown, R. L. (2014). African American men and women's attitudes toward mental illness, perceptions of stigma, and preferred coping behaviors. *Nursing Research, 62*(3), 185-194. Doi: 10.1097/NNR.0b013e31827bf533

Watkins, D. C. (2019). Improving the living, learning, and thriving of young Black men: A conceptual framework for reflection and projection. *International Journal of Environmental Research and Public Health, 16*(8)(1331), 1-13. Doi: 10.3390/ijerph16081331

Watson, J. (2024). Hear their voices: Black male student perceptions of retention initiatives at an HIS in the Midwest. *Dissertations, 851*, 1-170. https://digitalcommons.nl.edu/cgi/viewcontent.cgi?article=1914&context=diss

West, L. (2022). *The discussion of mental health in today's Black music*, 15 June. https://www.buzzfeed.com/lamarxwest/the-discussion-of-mental-health-in-todays-black-music

Western, B., & Sirois, C. (2018). Racialized re-entry: Labor market inequality after incarceration. Social Forces, 1-2. Doi: 10.1093/sf/soy096

What we do (2024). Black Men Teach. https://www.blackmenteach.org/what-we-do

Who we are (2024) 100 Black Men of America, Inc. https://100blackmen.org/who-we-are/

Who we are (2024). 100 Black Men of America, Inc. https://100blackmen.org/who-we-are/

Why we exist (2024). Black Male Voter Project. https://blackmalevoterproject.org/mission-and-vision/

Williams, D. R. (2003). The health of men: Structured inequalities and opportunities. *American Journal of Public Health, 93*(5), 724-731. Doi: 10.2105/ajph.93.5.724

Wilson, L. M. (2023). White politics, black lives, & the cost of being green: Environmental racism in Emelle, Alabama. *Midwest Social Sciences Journal, 26*(1)(10), 1-16. : https://doi.org/10.22543/2766-0796.1111

Wilson, M. N. (2004). *Parenting and parent-child interactions in African American families: A synopsis.* [University of Virginia: Charlottesville, VA], 1-4. https://prba.isr.umich.edu/wp-content/uploads/2024/06/MWilson.pdf

Wilson, N. (2018). Rap music as a positive influence on Black youth and American politics. *Advanced Writing: Pop Culture Intersections, 21,* 1-20. https://scholarcommons.sc u.edu/engl_176

Wingfield, A. H. (2014). Crossing the color line: Black professional men's development of interracial social networks. *Societies, 4,* 240-255. Doi: 10.3390/soc4020240

Wint, K. M., Opara, I., Gordon, R., & Brooms, D. R. (2022). Countering educational disparities among Black boys and Black adolescent boys from Pre-K to High School: A life course-intersectional perspective. *The Urban Review, 54,* 183-206. https://link.springer.com/article/10.1007/s11256-021-00616-z

Young, J. (2024). *More than a dozen Black billionaires live in the U.S., but only these four made the 2024 Forbes 400 list.* Forbes, 7 October. https://www.forbes.com/sites/jabariyoung/2024/10/02/this-tech-entrepreneur-is-the-richest-black-person-in-america/